BASEBALL
ARCHAEOLOGY

BASEBALL ARCHAEOLOGY

ARTIFACTS FROM THE GREAT AMERICAN PASTIME

Photography by Bret Wills

Text by Gwen Aldridge

CHRONICLE BOOKS

SAN FRANCISCO

A WMS BOOK

DESIGN: CRANBOURNE CHASE:
          DAVID MICKLEWRIGHT
          PAUL GARDNER

RESEARCH: BRAD SMITH

PRINTED IN JAPAN
ISBN 0-8118-0290-6 (PBK)
LIBRARY OF CONGRESS CATALOGING IN PUBLICATION DATA AVAILABLE

DISTRIBUTED IN CANADA BY RAINCOAST BOOKS
112 EAST THIRD AVENUE, VANCOUVER, B.C. V5T 1C8

10 9 8 7 6 5 4 3 2 1

CHRONICLE BOOKS
275 FIFTH STREET
SAN FRANCISCO, CA 94103

This book is dedicated to Dr. William A. Aldridge, loving father and good friend to us both.

Bret and Gwen.

ACKNOWLEDGMENTS

This book wouldn't have been possible without the help and generosity of the following people: Gary Van Allen and Peter Clark of the Baseball Hall of Fame, Bruce Dorskin, Tony Cocchi and Roger Pavey. Their knowledge and collections made this project a reality.

CONTENTS

7

Baseball is forever summer. Forever cut grass and chalk and the first awkward feel of a glove that's much too big. Even the casual observer can become caught up in a litany of associations: the murmur of stadiums, the perfect shape of a field, the carnival smell of hot dogs. Always, we are touched by baseball's unfailing innocence, its ability to conjure up the long golden days of a simpler time. Who wouldn't idealize it? Baseball is our childhood.

This is a book about artifacts — in particular, the artifacts associated with the playing and players of a century of baseball, from roughly 1880 to 1980. A loose dictionary definition of the word "artifact" is any object made by human work. What follows on these pages is a gallery of forms shaped and reshaped by the very human work of playing baseball. They are significant for the historical evolution of the objects themselves, and for their association with legends and legendary characters. They carry the form and feel of their time in a way no written word ever could. They are also objects that preserve and illuminate certain

GOLDEN AGE catcher's equipment.

aspects of America from before the turn of the last century on through the present time. With them we can follow the rise of an optimistic and naive game, its early refinement, and the emerging sophistication of equipment, players and fans. And as we dig, we notice the odd parallel between what was happening in the Great American Game and in America itself. Both game and country were blazing frontiers in the late 19th century. Each was enormously affected by the development of the media and mass communications. They shared a Golden Age and a Crash. And both grew up together from a loose confederation of local teams into vast, smoothly organized superstructures.

Certainly, it is more than poetic fancy that makes the coarse fabric of a uniform from the '20s somehow more real, more romantic, than the stretchy synthetics players wear today. A hand-engraved season pass somehow captures simple reverence for the game in a way a million computer-generated tickets never could. The old days weren't better, they were just simpler. And the objects from those times have a sweetness, a sort of clumsy beauty that reminds us of our country's youth. Of course, there is also the artistic element to be considered – that strange, subtle shift that can suddenly grace the most ordinary objects. This is something undoubtedly best left to the eye of the beholder. A catcher's mask from 1883 may remind you of the strong lines of a primitive war mask. Or not. To some, Babe Ruth's bowling ball is, in fact, just a bowling ball. To others, it's the perfect spherical metaphor for the great Bambino himself. Worn baseball gloves, creased and collapsing from decades of play, give us the shape of working hands, the imprints of lost games. And Robin Roberts' shoes capture a pitching style so intense, the outline of his footprint still remains in the leather.

WHITE SOX uniform on a Comiskey Park seat.

An object used by a famous person or in a famous deed takes on a life of its own. It has a power to intrigue that far outweighs portraits or autographs or autobiographies. Perhaps because artifacts have a unique way of reflecting the essentials of that person or that moment, they are physical, and they survive and hold time. The way they are put together, the care that was or wasn't taken to make them, the materials used, all tell us something. With them, we touch another time. We understand at a very human level how it was.

The philosopher Jacques Barzun once made a very wise observation: "Whoever wants to know the heart and mind of America had better learn baseball." This book chooses to explore some of "the heart and mind" by way of the cleat and plate. And with these unearthed remnants, we hope to find windows into ourselves and our past. This is the archaeology of baseball: picking up bits and pieces of the legends. Uncovering the bats and gloves and bases that made history, and putting them all together in a sequence of tangible evidence that reflects not only the culture of the sport, but also a bit of our own culture. Consider it a part of American history, as seen from the third base line.

9

THE EARLY YEARS

Chapter

I

THE EARLY YEARS

The real miracle of baseball is not, in fact, the '69 Mets. The real miracle of baseball is that the bases are exactly the right distance apart. We, of course, take this as a given, but mathematically and otherwise the design is without flaw. Any closer together, and scoring would be too easy. Any farther apart, practically impossible. All this has to do with achieving a perfect ratio between the velocity of the ball and human foot speed, but back in 1845, when Alexander Cartwright surveyed the first baseball field, these nuances of physics were not widely known or practiced. The invention of baseball has traditionally been credited to Civil War general Abner Doubleday. This is sentimental but misguided. Rudiments of the sport are clearly found in the British game of "rounders" and even farther back to a stick and ball game that was played in ancient Egypt. Certainly, the game received many of its official and long-standing refinements from Messrs. Cartwright and Doubleday. Cartwright specifically was responsible for the three-strike out, three outs to the inning and rules concerning foul balls.

Most of the important changes made to the game of baseball have had to do with improvements to the equipment. The evolution of the bat, refinements to the ball and the development of safety gear can be clearly traced during these early years. The first bats were thick, heavy and club-like. Often elaborately carved with team names, players' lucky numbers or nicknames, they would also inevitably be plastered with travel stickers like well-used steamer trunks. The primal fielder's glove, basically little more than a palm protector, was first worn in 1875 by Charles Waitt of St. Louis. Early gloves were not used for catching, but to stop the ball with the least amount of pain possible, while the other hand retrieved it. Exotic ideas such as webbing (1887) and padding (1918) didn't figure in until later. Eighteen-seventy-five was also the year the catcher's mask was invented by Fred Thayer. Basically a makeshift frame of thin metal wires attached to a leather facepiece, it beautifully illustrates how, in those days, very little was made to do quite a lot. Uniforms, also mostly improvised, were nevertheless developing certain themes and colors for specific teams. The New York Knickerbocker Club agreed in 1849 to dress their players in a costume consisting of blue woolen pantaloons, white flannel shirt and straw hat. Although this was generations away from Yankee pinstripe, the color blue would stick.

Team names would also undergo considerable evolution during these years. The Dodgers got their name from the hazardous nature of Brooklyn's trolley system, which was constantly making pedestrians dodge out of the way; before that, for reasons which escape us, they were known alternately as the Bridegrooms and the Superbas. Boston's Red Sox evolved out of early monikers including Speed Boys, Bean Eaters and Plymouth Rocks. And Chicago went through Colts, Orphans, Cowboys and Rainmakers before arriving at the final choice of Cubs.

Baseball in the years before 1900 was pretty much polite gang warfare. Fistfights on the field were commonplace. Broken fingers, smashed shins and assorted head injuries were reckoned part of the show. There is also considerable evidence that games were "sold" on a regular basis. Things being fast and loose as they were and players being mostly farm boys with empty pockets, it was easy for gamblers to slip a bit in here and there to see a game thrown. But amidst all the rudeness and ruffians, a few characters did rise up to become household names. The greatest of these was surely Rube Waddell. Rube used to pour ice water on his pitching arm to cool things down enough for the catcher to feel safe, hurl a few games, then disappear for a week to go fishing. Rube wrestled alligators in Florida, specialized in pub crawls and held up the start of many

of hard and furious fastballs. But in 1894, the distance from mound to home plate was increased to its present 60 feet, 6 inches, and Gleason became a hard and furious second baseman. And surely no roster would be complete without a mention of King Kelly, who started life as Michael Joseph Kelly, but was quickly elevated to royalty for his ability to play every position, and for his sensational base running. When Kelly was traded to the Boston Braves from the Chicago Cubs for a record $10,000, Chicago fans boycotted their own team. Except, of course, when Boston came to town, bringing Kelly with it.

No doubt about it, the early years were full of characters. If they were not widely known it was because mass

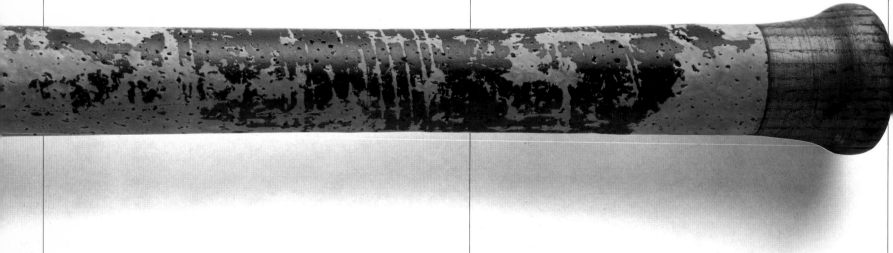

professional games by playing marbles with children outside the park. He was like a lot of other players of that time – basically a big kid who loved baseball. Another colorful character was Norman Elberfeld, also known as "The Tabasco Kid." Challenging base runners to spike him out of the way, the Kid had quite a collection of punctures, gouges and gashes on his tiny five-foot, five-inch frame. He would cauterize each new addition (still poised on the base) with raw whiskey. Then there was Kid Gleason, probably best known as the betrayed manager of the notorious Black Sox. In the early 1890s, Gleason was a pitcher

communication, making possible the immediate spread of scores and plays, was still in its infancy. The most famous heroes of this early age were limited in exposure to the actual numbers of fans the team park could hold. Annoying as this was, it did keep the game for the few and true, and instead of by television and radio publicity, the players were memorialized by the fans in other ways. Anyone looking back at the souvenirs of the time – the highly detailed tobacco cards, the hand-tinted players' album, the elaborate programs and pins and medals – begins to understand the early fans' extraordinary devotion to the sport of baseball.

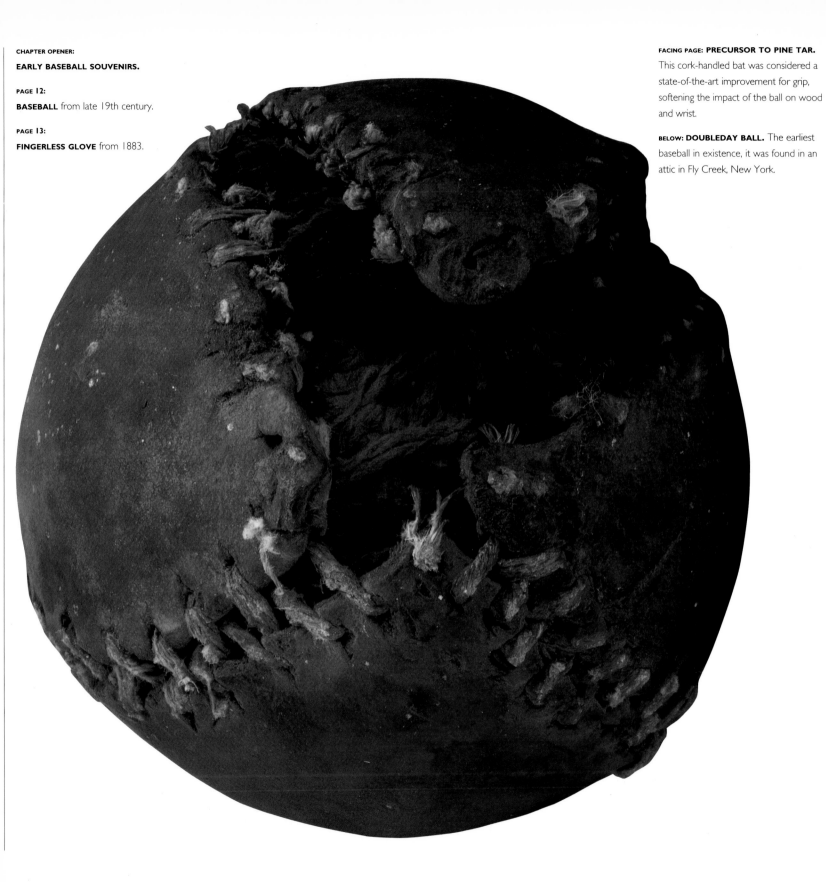

CHAPTER OPENER:

EARLY BASEBALL SOUVENIRS.

PAGE 12:

BASEBALL from late 19th century.

PAGE 13:

FINGERLESS GLOVE from 1883.

FACING PAGE: **PRECURSOR TO PINE TAR.**
This cork-handled bat was considered a
state-of-the-art improvement for grip,
softening the impact of the ball on wood
and wrist.

BELOW: **DOUBLEDAY BALL.** The earliest
baseball in existence, it was found in an
attic in Fly Creek, New York.

15

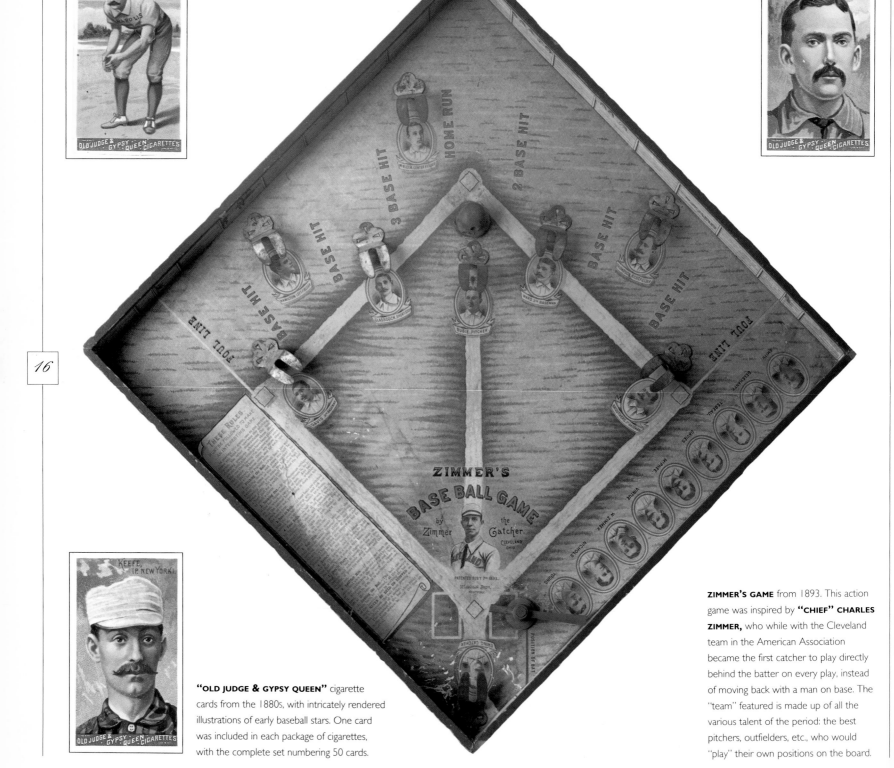

"OLD JUDGE & GYPSY QUEEN" cigarette cards from the 1880s, with intricately rendered illustrations of early baseball stars. One card was included in each package of cigarettes, with the complete set numbering 50 cards.

ZIMMER'S GAME from 1893. This action game was inspired by **"CHIEF" CHARLES ZIMMER,** who while with the Cleveland team in the American Association became the first catcher to play directly behind the batter on every play, instead of moving back with a man on base. The "team" featured is made up of all the various talent of the period: the best pitchers, outfielders, etc., who would "play" their own positions on the board.

BOSTON BASEBALL ASSOCIATION SEASON PASS from 1871.

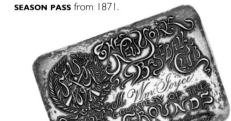

SILVER SEASON PASSES.

THE ROUND ALBUM was a tobacco premium from Goodwin & Co. in the early 1880s. Each cigarette package contained a coupon redeemable for gifts. After collecting 100 of them, fans would receive this beautifully colored collection of famous early players of the National League, including **CAP ANSON, TIM KEEFE** and **JOHN M. WARD,** all future Hall of Famers.

BELOW: GEORGE VAN HALTREN'S trophy bat from the **NEW YORK NATIONAL LEAGUE** team, in 1898.

BELOW: Intricately carved bat from the late 1890s **BLUE STOCKINGS** team.

No single piece of baseball equipment has undergone as many changes as the glove. From its initial appearance as a palm protector, through numerous incarnations, ending in today's heavily padded, webbed and laced designs, form has always been in hot pursuit of function. Given the basic tasks of scooping, catching, surrounding or trapping, gloves have mutated into complex leather nets capable of adding reach and reducing error. From 1845 to about 1874 players worked bare-handed, and shattered fingers, mashed palms and sprained wrists were common. Early gloves simply improved the grip and took some of the sting out of a catch. They were thin, fingerless, unpadded creations with limited shock-absorbing ability and required two-handed catches. Webbing between thumb and forefinger was not added until the turn of the century, when players realized how much trapping and holding ability would be increased if that open space in the hand was blocked. In 1918 Bill Doak of the Cardinals tried out a cushioned design with a built-up heel that formed a V-pocket. This one change so improved Doak's catching that the word spread and soon all kinds of variations in heel padding and pockets began showing up. Modern gloves are larger and wider compared with the early models. Babe Ruth's glove was scarcely bigger than his hand, and makes today's over-sized variety seem as big as a grocery bag. Gloves also vary according to the specific positions they assist: a vast, pillow-like mitt for the catcher, a huge leather scoop for the first baseman, fully closed, grip-concealing gloves for the pitcher, a loosely worn webbed net for the infielder and flexible, fly-snapping handgear for the outfielder. Without question, the glove is the most personalized item of equipment a baseball player has, and his "gamer" is kept faithfully until it falls apart or until somebody steals it.

1883 FINGERLESS GLOVE.

1988 OUTFIELDER'S GL

1982 FIRST BASEMAN'S GLOVE.

1900–05 PADDED HEEL GLOVE.

1884 CATCHER'S MITT WITH
INDEPENDENT FINGERS AND
NO WEBBING.

1910 WEBBED GLOVE.

1979 CATCHER'S MITT.

1950 WEBBED AND LACED GLOVE.

20

LEFT: MEDAL given to **MIKE "KING" KELLY** by a fan named Nuf Ced McGreevey, honoring his base-stealing ability in 1887, the season when **BOSTON** bought him for the unheard-of amount of $10,000.

ABOVE: FAN PIN from the **BOSTON "RED STOCKINGS."**

ABOVE LEFT: HANDMADE MEDAL honoring **WILLIAM "BUCK" EWING,** who was a deadball era National League home run champ. In 1883 he hit 10 for **NEW YORK** and was honored with this award.

ABOVE: DAUVRAY CUP PIN. An in-house award given by **DETROIT** to the most valuable player of its team.

RIGHT: SOUVENIR PORTRAIT PIN, featuring the **BALTIMORE ORIOLES** of 1894.

ABOVE: EARLY MEDAL. A "rooter's" (loud, active fan) pin with "Beantown" emblem suspended from handmade fabric flag.

STOCK CERTIFICATE for the **PHILADELPHIA BASEBALL CLUB,** at the then very expensive rate of $50 a share.

1888 SCORECARD. The **CINCINNATI CLUB** always featured a team member on the cover. Since the club had 24 members and played more than 24 games a season, it was prone to repeats.

1889 WORLD TOUR LUNCHEON PROGRAM. A missionary effort funded by **ALBERT G. SPALDING** in the interest of promoting baseball worldwide, the tour included exhibition games in New Zealand, Australia, Ceylon, Egypt, the Sandwich Islands (now Hawaii), Italy, France and England. Stars such as **ADRIAN C. ANSON** and **JOHN M. WARD** played on such varied turf as football fields, race courses and in this case a cricket ground. In addition to the English royalty present on this occasion, the players would meet various crowned heads such as King Humbert and Prince Borghese of Italy and King Kakakuaau of Hawaii.

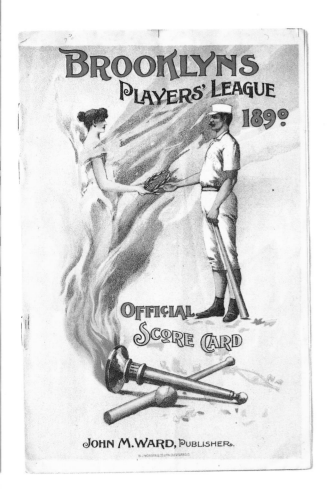

PLAYERS LEAGUE PROGRAM.
In the last years of the 1880s, labor problems between owners and players led to the formation of a third league, the short-lived Players League. **JOHN M. WARD,** featured on the program cover, was founder and president.

There is something very warlike about this piece of defensive equipment. Essentially a cage for the face, the catcher's mask is a distant descendant of English fencing headgear, with the object being to protect the face and eyes from foreign objects intruding at high speed. But as the tip of a foil carries considerably less impact than a five-ounce ball traveling at speeds up to 90 miles an hour, the catcher's mask developed steel ribs instead of mesh, and an open framework design that allowed the catcher unimpeded visibility. The first mask was designed in 1875 by Fred Thayer, who played for Harvard. Up to that time, catchers played completely without protection, and broken jaws, noses and teeth were considered occupational hazards. Over time, various design changes would include reinforced bars at the most common impact points (forehead and nose), reconfigured ribs to increasingly improve visibility, and the addition of a throat protector.

1885 MASK.

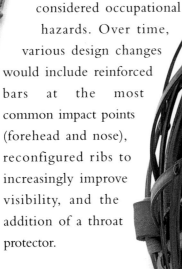

1875 FRED THAYER MASK.

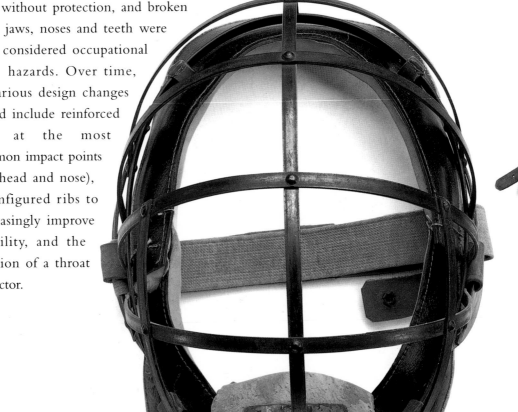

1878 HOWLAND MASK.

1883 MASK.

1970 MASK.

1936
MICKEY COCHRANE MASK.

1979
STEVE YEAGER MASK WITH A
THROAT PROTECTOR.

1941
MICKEY OWEN MASK.

1988
CARLTON FISK MASK.

THE DEADBALL ERA

ERA

Chapter

II

THE DEADBALL ERA

Deadballs don't fly — they thunk. A loosely wrapped core with little overall resilience kept the action primarily in the infield. Games were characterized by rough and tumble tactics, with plays pushed as far outside the rules as players could manage. It was a time of precision bunts and base stealing, of power slides and sharpened cleats and anything goes, just get the run in. Pitchers aimed to hit the batter. Batters aimed to bomb the infield. And base runners were more than happy to rob, cheat or batter the basemen. It was a lively game, basically a cross between ballet and barroom brawling. Not to imply the age lacked finesse — early players insisted their method of place hitting required more skill and strategy than the "pop 'em out of the stadium" plays of later days.

Innovations and improvements to the equipment were directly related to the turbulent style of the game. Glove design began to feature substantial padding and webbing in an attempt to protect the hand from the ball, and trap the ball more securely. Protective equipment such as the first shin guard (1907) and first safety cup (1916) just naturally evolved in a game where heavily spiked shoes were constantly introducing themselves to someone's lower body. This was also the age of the great parks. Ebbets, Fenway, Wrigley,

Comiskey, Shibe all rose up between 1910 and 1914 to replace the early, smaller pastures with their bring-your-own-chair arrangements. In time, the great temples of baseball would themselves become celebrities, revered for their individual peculiarities and playing fields.

Although the game was still young, the souvenir and advertising industry were by this time well developed. Baseball cards offered as premiums with cigarettes and Cracker Jacks were especially popular. Players appeared on all kinds of souvenir pins and pennants, and could be found hawking everything from tobacco to sock garters. A new magazine, "Baseball," was introduced in 1911 to immediate success. And baseball cap collections were the order of the day.

On the field there was plenty to hold your attention. Eddie Collins of the Chicago Cubs, with 743 lifetime stolen bases, ran the paths like a fox terrier: fake and return, fly and slide. Brooklyn Dodger Wee Willie Keeler, another base burglar extraordinaire, was often quoted on the subject of his advice to batters, "Keep your eye on the ball and hit 'em where they ain't." And of course, there was the great Tyrus Raymond Cobb, the most watchable and least likable figure in the history of baseball. A curious mixture of great talent and gross arrogance, Cobb had a drive to

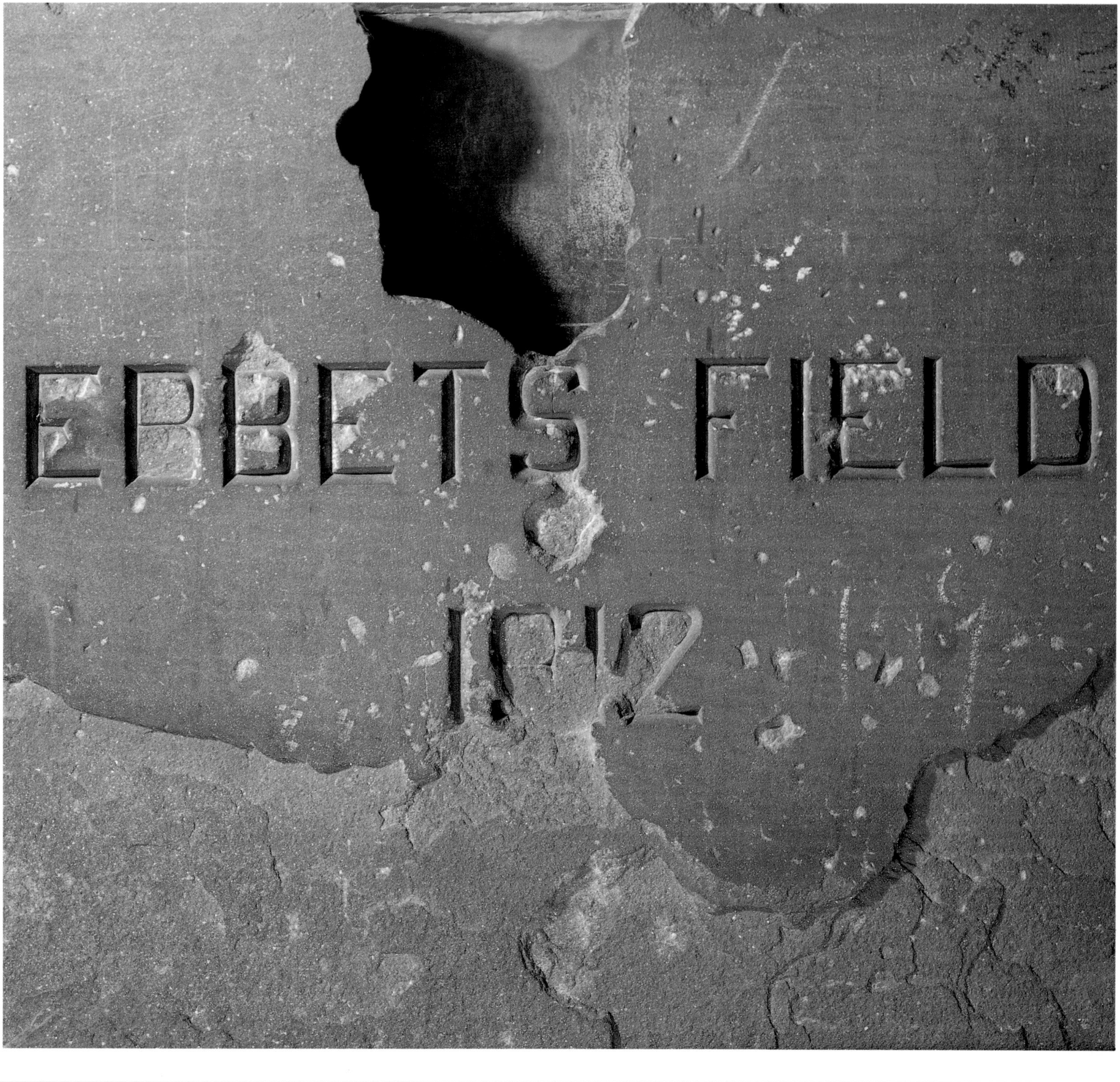
EBBETS FIELD

succeed that bordered on maniacal. One of his favorite pre-game warm-up exercises was to pick a prominent place in the dugout and start sharpening his spikes in full view of opposing infielders. As he was known for a "spikes high" style of sliding, this action would certainly make anyone think twice about getting in his way on the base paths. Also known for a somewhat cold-blooded approach to winning was fiery third baseman John McGraw. Famous in later years as the great manager and strategist for the New York Giants, McGraw spent his early years blocking, tripping and hooking the belts of those unfortunate base runners who happened his way. At the other end of the spectrum was Christy Mathewson, a gentleman and a scholar at a time in baseball when such qualities were rarer than triple plays. An advertiser's dream – tall, blond and blue-eyed – Mathewson was the one primarily responsible for elevating the game out of its cussing and kicking stages to a more dignified national sport. Another favorite was that pipe-smoking, log-splitting pioneer of pitchers, Denton "Cy" Young, who collected an extraordinary 511 major league wins over 22 seasons. In 1908 a crowd of 20,000 watched as the "Boston Post" presented Cy with a four-foot trophy honoring his hurl. It was the first of many Cy Young awards. Upholding infield glory were the fabled combo Joe Tinker, Johnny Evers and Frank Chance. A trio so smooth, so relentless in their handling of double plays, they were committed to memory forever by way of a little ditty by newspaper columnist and Giants fan Franklin P. Adams, which begins:

These are the saddest of possible words –

Tinker to Evers to Chance.

Trio of Bear Cubs and fleeter than birds

Tinker to Evers to Chance.

All in all, it was an age of hit and run. Games were played close to the bases, with the infield often determining the success of a team.

CHAPTER OPENER: **TURNSTILE** from **COMISKEY PARK,** home of the **CHICAGO WHITE SOX.**

PAGE 26: **LOOSELY WOUND DEADBALL** from 1909.

PAGE 27: **CORNERSTONE** from **EBBETS FIELD,** Brooklyn, New York.

BELOW: Three issues of **"BASEBALL MAGAZINE."**

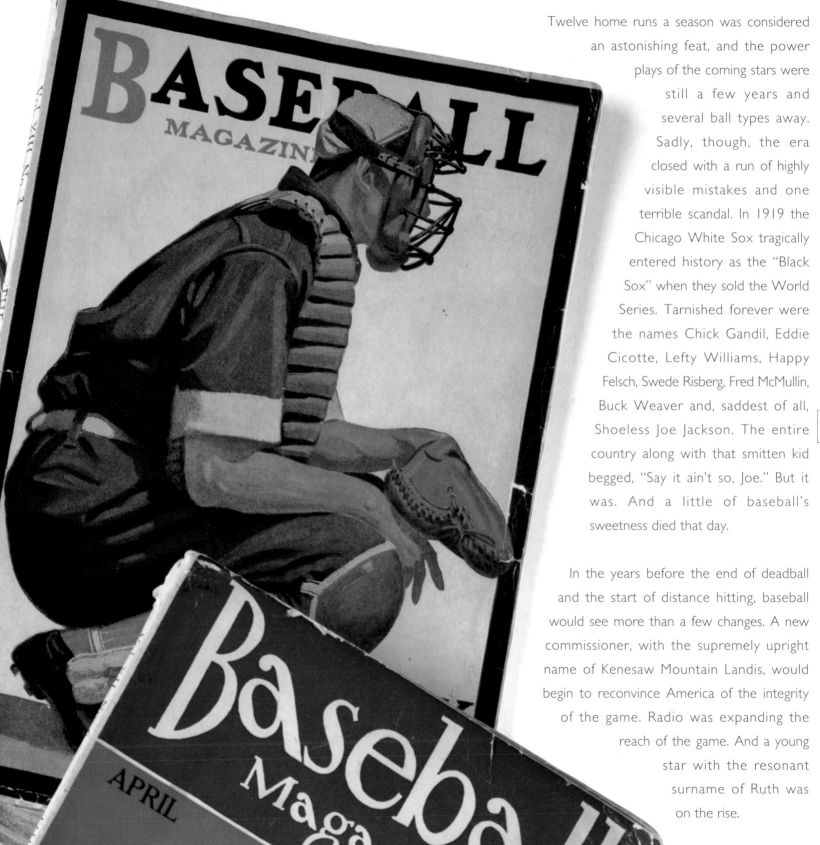

Twelve home runs a season was considered an astonishing feat, and the power plays of the coming stars were still a few years and several ball types away. Sadly, though, the era closed with a run of highly visible mistakes and one terrible scandal. In 1919 the Chicago White Sox tragically entered history as the "Black Sox" when they sold the World Series. Tarnished forever were the names Chick Gandil, Eddie Cicotte, Lefty Williams, Happy Felsch, Swede Risberg, Fred McMullin, Buck Weaver and, saddest of all, Shoeless Joe Jackson. The entire country along with that smitten kid begged, "Say it ain't so, Joe." But it was. And a little of baseball's sweetness died that day.

In the years before the end of deadball and the start of distance hitting, baseball would see more than a few changes. A new commissioner, with the supremely upright name of Kenesaw Mountain Landis, would begin to reconvince America of the integrity of the game. Radio was expanding the reach of the game. And a young star with the resonant surname of Ruth was on the rise.

CY YOUNG'S 1908 PITCHING AWARD. Long before the **CY YOUNG** award (given every year since 1956 to the best pitcher in baseball) came this Cy Young award, given to the great pitcher by the readers of the "Boston Post."

COMMEMORATIVE BASEBALL CARD autographed by Young, whose actual first name was Denton, but who adopted the "Cy" in the 1890s after a young catcher in the minor leagues judged him to be "fast as a cyclone."

BASEBALL'S GREAT
HALL OF FAME

Cleveland N.L. 1890-98, St. Louis N.L. 1899-1900; Boston A.L. 1901-08, Cleveland A.L. 1909-11; Boston N.L. 1911. Only pitcher in first 100 years of baseball to win 500 games. Among his 511 wins were 3 no-hit shutouts. Pitched perfect game May 5, 1904.   AN EXHIBIT CARD

AUTOGRAPHED KINDLING. Young credited his off-season farm work, which included chopping wood and doing heavy chores, with keeping him in shape for 22 seasons in baseball. This piece was taken from a pile chopped in early November 1954, several months before Young's 88th birthday.

PIPE AND CASE. Off the mound, **CY YOUNG** was always seen chewing on a pipe.

CY YOUNG AUTOGRAPHED BALL AND CAP.

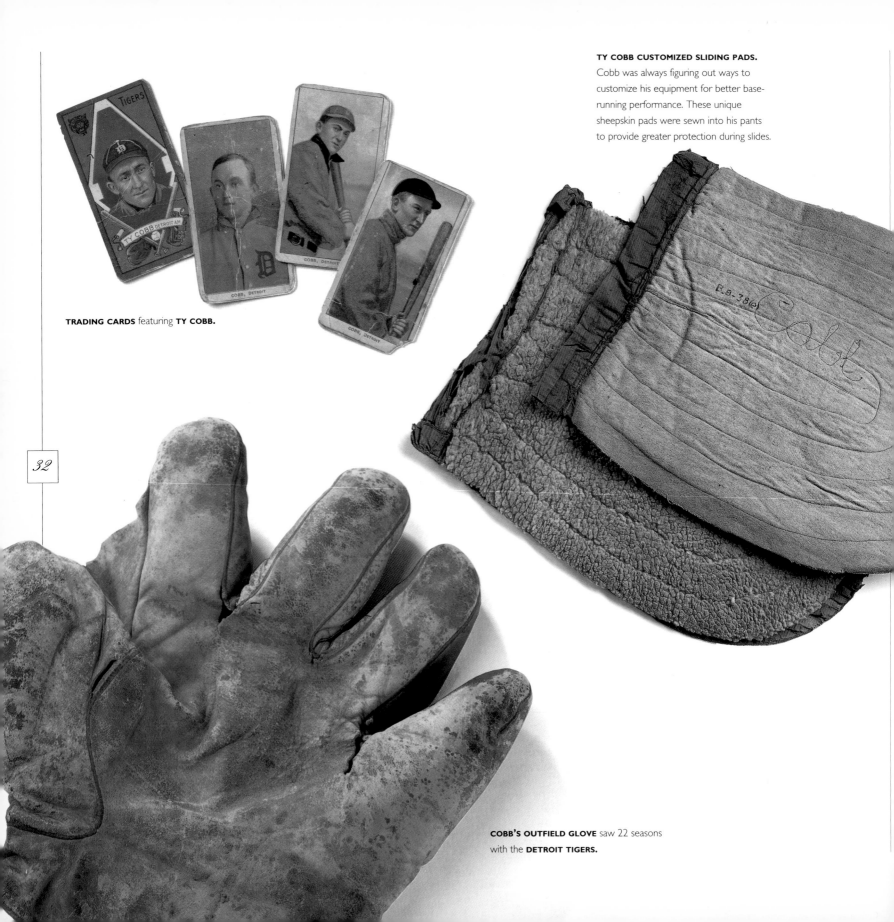

TY COBB CUSTOMIZED SLIDING PADS.
Cobb was always figuring out ways to customize his equipment for better base-running performance. These unique sheepskin pads were sewn into his pants to provide greater protection during slides.

TRADING CARDS featuring **TY COBB.**

COBB'S OUTFIELD GLOVE saw 22 seasons with the **DETROIT TIGERS.**

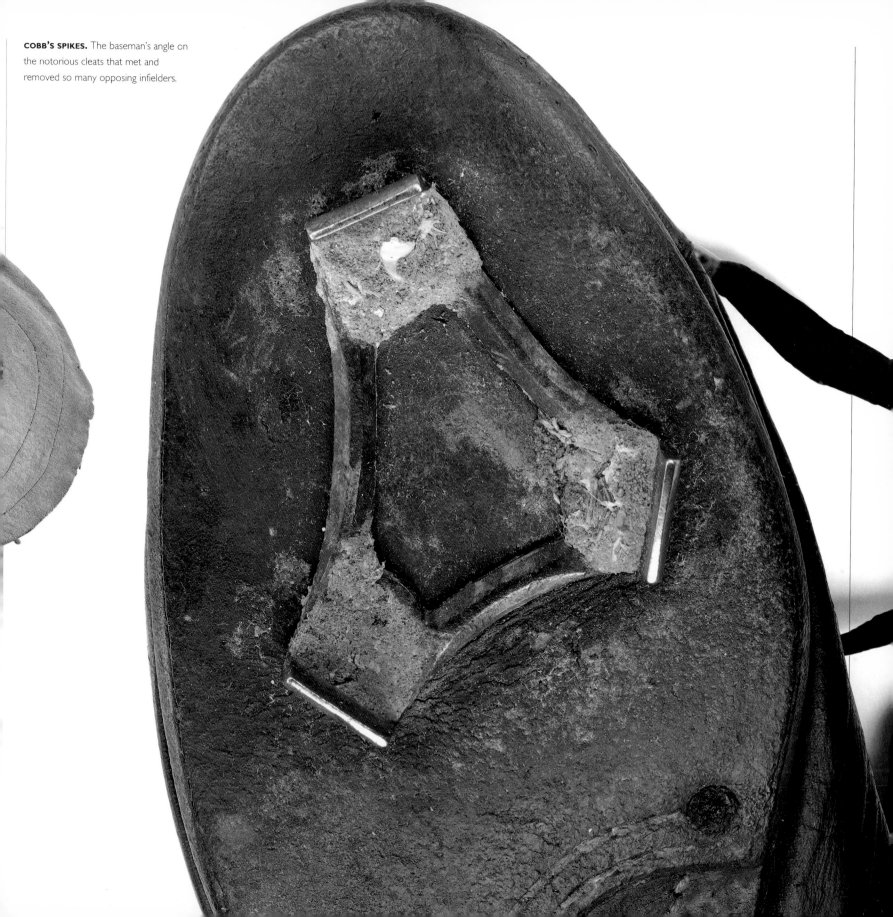

COBB'S SPIKES. The baseman's angle on the notorious cleats that met and removed so many opposing infielders.

BALL EVOLUTION

The evolution of the ball has essentially determined the evolution of the game. Changes in its construction have had immediate effects on the way baseball is played. Early balls had little rebound and didn't often go beyond the confines of the park. Consequently, early baseball was a choke up and punch affair. Players relied heavily on hit and run, bunting and large holes in the infield. After 1910, the more tightly wound "rabbit balls" began to show up in the leagues, and with a far greater capacity for springing over fences and out of the park, the new pills ushered in the age of power baseball. Home runs and the men who could hit them became much more the point of the sport. Through all the changes in core and tension, the baseball has varied relatively little in size (nine to nine and a quarter inches in circumference) and weight (five ounces to five and a quarter ounces). Essentially, the ball is a cork-covered sphere, with two layers of rubber wrapped by 219 yards of wool yarn, 150 yards of cotton yarn, sealed by a coating of rubber cement, given a cover of tanned cowhide, all held in place by exactly 216 stitches. The ball stitcher pictured at left has remained standard equipment in the industry up to modern times. All of the balls used today by major league teams are produced by the Rawlings Sporting Goods Company and are made in Haiti.

1839 DOUBLEDAY BALL.

1908 DEADBALL ERA BALL.

1988 AMERICAN LEAGUE CORK CUSHIONED BALL.

1858 REGULATION BALL.

1855 SMALL ONE-PIECE-COVER BALL.

1868 ONE–PIECE-COVER BALL.

1890 SEAMLESS-COVER BALL.

1876 DOUBLE 8 COVER BALL.

LENA BLACKBURNE MUD, used to take the polish off balls before play.

WELCOME HOME RIBBON for the World Tourists, an exhibition team made up of **WHITE SOX** and **GIANTS** players, whose globe-trotting tour included Japan, France and Italy.

RECEPTION COMMITTEE

WELCOME HOME
COMISKEY
Mc. GRAW
CALLAHAN
AND
WORLD'S TOURISTS

"SHOELESS" JOE JACKSON'S shoes, from his days with the infamous 1919 **CHICAGO WHITE SOX.**

EDDIE
COTTE

1909 WORLD CHAMPIONS PIN.

SEASON PASSES. Ranging from the ornate metal engraving of 1902 to the more pedestrian cardboard versions of 1911.

TROPHY WATCH carried by EDDIE CICOTTE, pitcher for the WHITE SOX, who helped to throw the 1919 World Series.

JOHNNY EVERS' GLOVE. Used by the CHICAGO CUBS second baseman to earn the nickname of "Crab," for the way he sidled up to ground balls.

THE FIRST KNOWN SAFETY CUP. A solid steel device thankfully worn by catcher **CLAUDE BERRY** in 1916.

EARLY PLAYERS' CONTRACT, for **NAPOLEON RUCKER,** pitcher for the **BROOKLYN DODGERS,** who was considered one of the best of his time (1907–16) and consequently received a princely $3,000 a year.

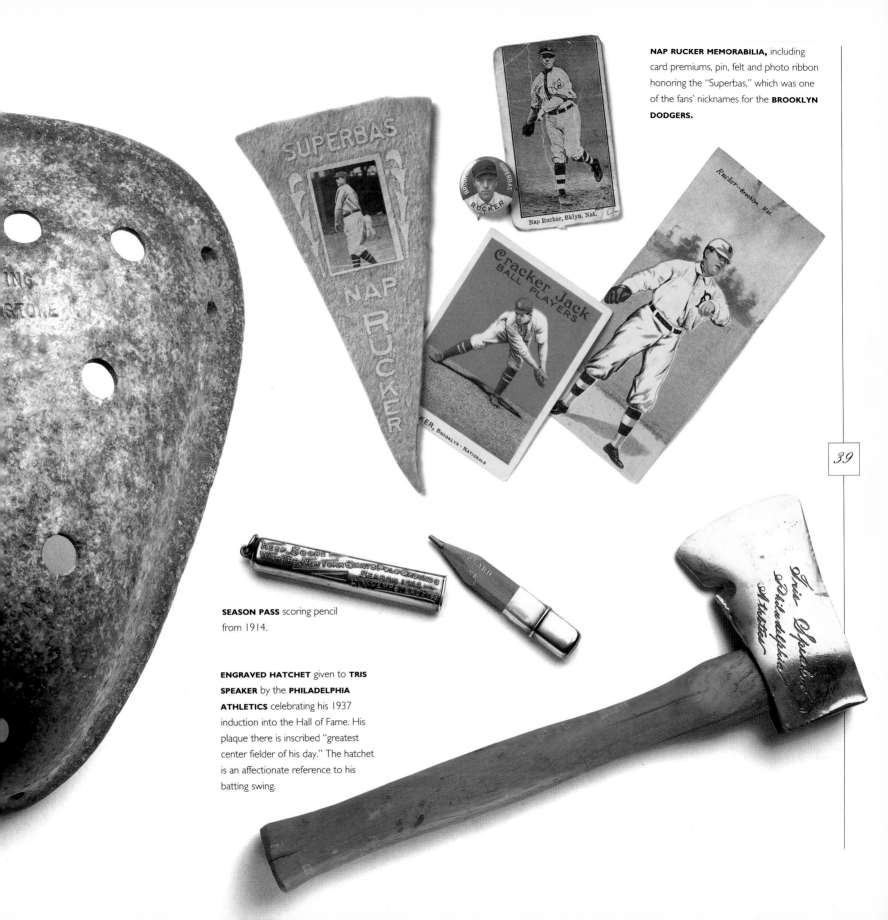

NAP RUCKER MEMORABILIA, including card premiums, pin, felt and photo ribbon honoring the "Superbas," which was one of the fans' nicknames for the **BROOKLYN DODGERS.**

SEASON PASS scoring pencil from 1914.

ENGRAVED HATCHET given to **TRIS SPEAKER** by the **PHILADELPHIA ATHLETICS** celebrating his 1937 induction into the Hall of Fame. His plaque there is inscribed "greatest center fielder of his day." The hatchet is an affectionate reference to his batting swing.

FAR LEFT: **TEAM SCORECARD** from 1910. Included in the lineup of this minor league team from Shelbyville, Tennessee, was young **CHARLES DILLON STENGEL,** an outfielder still two years away from the majors and the nickname "Casey," after his hometown of Kansas City.

BOTTOM LEFT: **INTRICATELY EMBROIDERED SILK PATCH,** circa 1910, from the **NEW YORK BASEBALL LEAGUE.**

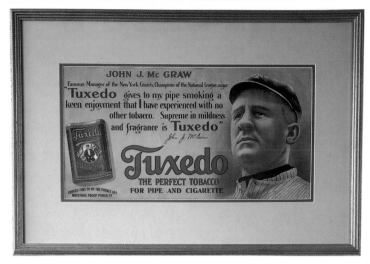

LEFT: **STREETCAR ADVERTISEMENT FOR TUXEDO TOBACCO,** featuring **JOHN McGRAW.** Interesting because "mildness" is certainly not one of the qualities his teammates would have attributed to "Little Napoleon."

BELOW: **GEORGE LEVY'S MEGAPHONE.** Before radio, microphones and public address systems, scores and player information were relayed through the stands by way of one man with a megaphone. George Levy was one of the more long-winded of these announcers, with a career extending from 1900 to 1940. He announced both Giants and Yankees games.

NEAL BALL'S GLOVE. Notable for its performance in 1909 when Ball fielded major league's first unassisted triple play against the Red Sox. Only one season before, the **CLEVELAND INDIANS** infielder led American League shortstops with 80 errors.

THE FEDERAL LEAGUE

JOE TINKER

CHIFEDS

The early 20th century was a great time in American history for trust-busting and monopoly-breaking, and out of this expansionist spirit came the concept of a Federal League. Founded by John T. Powers and other entrepreneurs in 1913, the Federal League proposed that baseball's ever-growing popularity could support a third major league. In its first year the six-team circuit kept a low profile and respected major league contracts. Although all six managers were former players of some note (including Cy Young), the teams themselves were made up mostly of unknowns and a few has-been ex-majors. In 1914, however, the Federal League expanded to eight teams and put franchises in eastern cities. This marked the beginning of confrontation with the already existing NL and AL. In principle, the FL was still respecting the major leagues' contracts, but an abundance of players looking to increase their salaries led to deals with the FL that were perceived by the other two leagues as out-and-out theft. Several prominent players went over, including Joe Tinker and Mordecai Brown, which stirred up further warfare in court and in the press. In the end, litigation was responsible for ending the Federal League's brief existence. Although it had fair attendance and a close race for its pennant, the financial burdens of continual lawsuits proved too costly. By the winter of 1915, the Federal League had folded.

ABOVE: **FEDERAL LEAGUE PENNANT,** featuring **JOE TINKER,** and **FEDERAL LEAGUE SCOREBOOKS.**

ROGER BRESNAHAN'S BAT from 1905 when he played for the **GIANTS.** Although that year he hit .302, Bresnahan was most noted for his experiments in safety equipment, including a prototype leather batting helmet and the first catcher's shin guards.

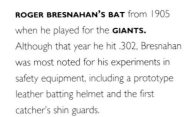

SEASON PASSES from **NEW YORK BASEBALL CLUB** in 1908.

ADVERTISING AND BASEBALL get together in Boston. Illustrated scorecards became a convenient way to bring in extra income to support teams as well as encourage fans to keep up with the stats.

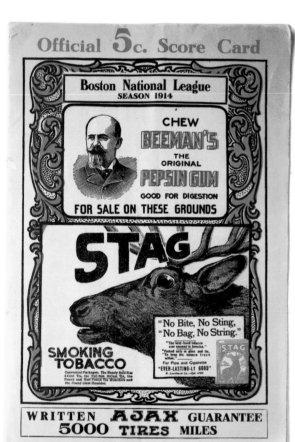

ILLUSTRATED SPORTING NEWS issue from 1904, celebrating **DEACON McGUIRE,** who appeared in more major league seasons than any catcher in history (26) and caught in over 1,700 games.

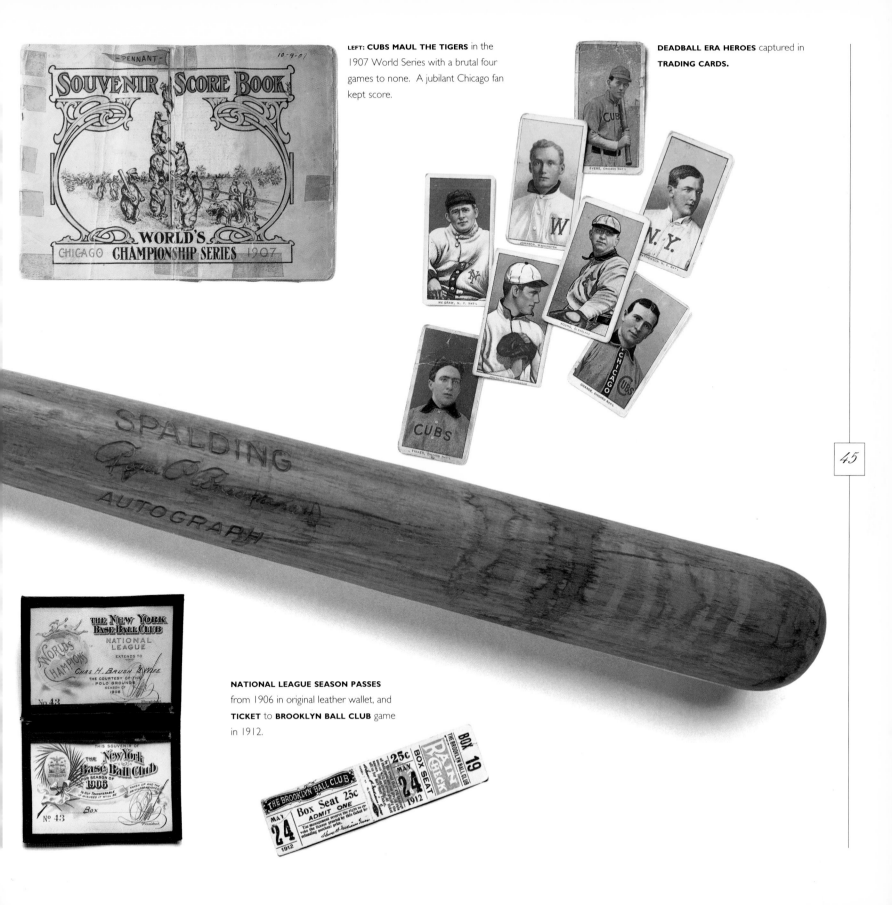

LEFT: CUBS MAUL THE TIGERS in the 1907 World Series with a brutal four games to none. A jubilant Chicago fan kept score.

DEADBALL ERA HEROES captured in **TRADING CARDS.**

NATIONAL LEAGUE SEASON PASSES from 1906 in original leather wallet, and **TICKET** to **BROOKLYN BALL CLUB** game in 1912.

WORLD SERIES PRESS PINS for the **PHILADELPHIA ATHLETICS** granting access to press seating in Shibe Park. The elephant is a traditional mascot of the Athletics and has stayed with them through their various incarnations: the Philadelphia A's, Kansas City A's and Oakland A's.

TINKER TO EVERS TO CHANCE by way of Tinker's shoes, Evers' glove and Chance's bat. All from the 1900–16 period.

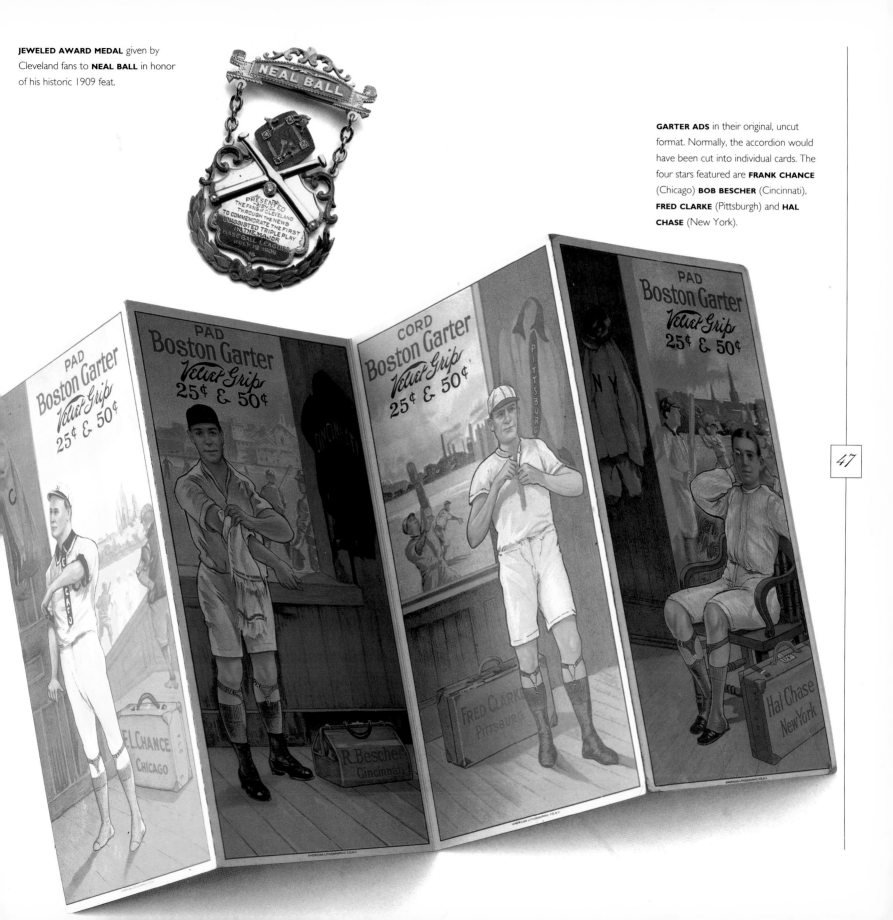

JEWELED AWARD MEDAL given by Cleveland fans to **NEAL BALL** in honor of his historic 1909 feat.

GARTER ADS in their original, uncut format. Normally, the accordion would have been cut into individual cards. The four stars featured are **FRANK CHANCE** (Chicago) **BOB BESCHER** (Cincinnati), **FRED CLARKE** (Pittsburgh) and **HAL CHASE** (New York).

47

SONGBOOKS

t's been said that if you want to know what's on America's mind, just listen to what she's singing. It would seem, given the vast amount of sheet music and songs produced during this period, that America was thinking a lot about baseball. Specifically, about the grandeur of green, the heroics of the lonely outfielder and why all umpires should be shot. Perhaps most popular were the piano arrangements of various teams' entrance marches. Long before the organ music modern fans associate with baseball came these marching band fanfares. Each team had its own special song, and true fans could not only whistle the refrain, they could produce children able to pick out the melody on the family upright.

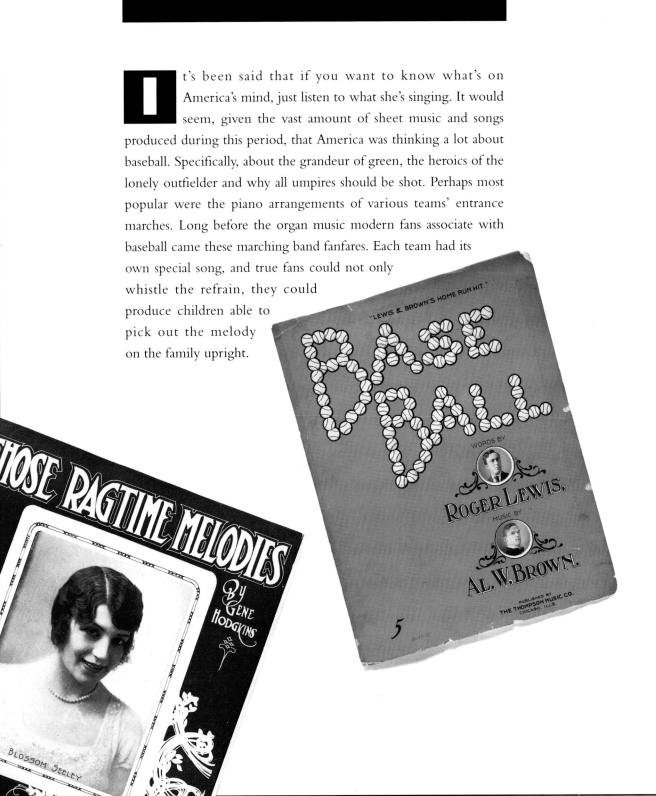

ARCH SONG "HIT"

OLD
ME
BALL

onnor

R Co-Boston

DEDICATED TO CHARLES A. COMISKEY.

THE
WHITE SOX
MARCH

1907

WORLD'S CHAMPIONS · AMERICAN LEAGUE CHAMPIONS

5

By T.F. Durand,
COMPOSER OF
TWINKLING STARS

Thomas F. Douthar,
MUSIC PUBLISHER
516 W. Chicago Av., Chicago, Ill.

REMEMBER ME TO
MY OLD GAL

SUCCESSFULLY INTRODUCED BY
THOSE THREE GREAT BALL PLAYERS,
CHIEF BENDER, COOMBS
AND MORGAN
THE HEROES OF THE
WORLD'S SERIES

WORDS BY
GEORGE MORIARITY
CAPTAIN OF THE DETROIT BASE-BALL TEAM
MUSIC BY
AL.W. BROWN AND J. BRANDON WALSH

AT THE BALL GAME

for the
piano

by
OLOF THUNSTROM

THE GOLDEN AGE

Chapter

III

THE GOLDEN AGE

By the 1920s, America was deep into a love affair with baseball. For most males of the era it was as essential a topic as the weather and what was for dinner. No self-respecting gentleman would allow himself to be caught without the proper conversational ammunition for debating all the merits of that day's game. Whether making a pilgrimage to the park, or following line scores as they were updated in the afternoon dailies, it was imperative to stay on top of the plays. Unlike most of the other sporting events of the era, baseball was very much a communal experience. Families went together. Companies went together. Entire neighborhoods hunkered down around their radios to listen as Graham MacNamee announced the World Series. Clearly the game had grabbed the nation in a way normally reserved for wars and presidential elections. Like a rough backwoods rowdy who decides one day it's time for a sweetheart, professional baseball had cleaned itself up, gone out courting and won the heart of the American public.

Who could resist investing a nickel for that season's scorecards? And having invested, who would dare to miss even one pitch, hit or run? People were statistics crazy. Record crazy. World Series crazy. Souvenir crazy. At home or in the park, fans treasured elaborate silver season passes, scoring pencils,

rooters' pins and pennants. Medals, even crowns, were made to honor the heroes of the moment. This was more than a game. This was creeping close to a religion, complete with all the attendant rituals and reliquaries. Baseball was the national pastime. It was our sport, as uniquely American as cowboys, bubble gum or the Constitution. This was the game in its Golden Age – no longer disreputable, though still a little rough around the edges. The rabbit ball was loose in the leagues, baseball had its first commissioner, and the Yankee dynasty that would dominate the game for nearly 45 years was lining up. It was a time of kings and clowns and heroes. Even the names sound like something out of folklore: Goose Goslin, Dizzy Dean, Mule Haas, Van Lingle Mungo, Lefty Grove, Heinie Manush, Travis Jackson, Cornelius McGillicuddy, Muddy Ruel. And, of course, the moniker to end all monikers – George Herman Ruth.

More than anyone or anything else, this enormous personality brought baseball off the back lot and into the spotlight. At first glance, he was not an easy hero, with a moon face, matchstick legs and a girth that said more about beer and sandwiches than it did about baseball. But oh, the swing, that magic, fluid sweep that

seemed to hang in space for a heartbeat before it sent the ball crashing through legend after legend. There was not, nor ever will be, anything quite like the Babe – exuberant, extravagant, rebellious, childish, Babe was the embodiment of his era. In a sport that was never short of characters, the "Bambino" was unique in his ability to do the right thing at the right time. Whether it was calling that homer (as legend has it) of the '27 Series or patiently signing autographs for fans on anything and everything, Babe was a PR natural. As his celebrity grew, so did the prestige he brought to the sport.

Teams of this period played a game that basically hasn't changed up through modern times. What they wore and what they were playing it with, however, was another matter entirely. Uniforms were thick woolen affairs that drooped in the drawers and itched all summer. The baggy knickers helped hide some of the less-than-svelte figures found gracing the fields. In fact, the trademark Yankee pinstripe was originally adopted in the early '20s to camouflage Babe Ruth's ballooning waistline (almost 50 inches by 1925). Gloves were much smaller, except for the catcher's mitt, which was proportioned along the lines of a leather telephone book. Caps were flatter and batting helmets

55

unheard of, which might explain why early players feared "bean balls" far more than the deadliest curve. The early days saw a variety of illegal pitches that defied description and quite often the batter. There was the spitball, the shine ball, the dirt ball, the emery ball, the greaseball, the eyelet ball and the notorious coffee ball (unscrupulous pitchers chewed coffee beans and spat into the seams). To think about Gehrig or Ruth hitting the averages they did, against some of the pitches they got, makes the records even more impressive.

Fans were also a different breed, perhaps because attending a game meant so much more then. It was a thing to be looked forward to for weeks ahead, and relived in the memory a long time after. And since the only place to really see the players was on the field, their heroic proportions were more easily preserved. The press of the time was a willing participant in the illusion, and thus few candid interviews and newspaper exposés, and no public contract disputes, meant fans were free to enjoy their champions without all the tarnishing personal details. Maybe this is the real reason we think of the 1920s as the Golden Age of baseball — it was the age of unimpeded romanticism.

KING CARL'S CROWN. A screwballer of royal proportions, **CARL HUBBELL** was revered by fans for his singular but highly effective pitching style. Powering the Giants from 1928 to 1943 with his corkscrew windup and stupefying screwball pitch, Hubbell was dubbed "king" by the fans and given this crowning honor by Seagrams when voted into the Hall of Fame in 1947.

PORTRAIT OF THE "KING," as preserved in a 1936 **NY GIANTS** souvenir pin.

GEORGIA RED. Crimson clay from the boyhood field of **JOHNNY MIZE,** who grew up to become a strong, burly slugger for the Cardinals, Giants and Yankees and the only man to hit three home runs in a game, six times.

MICKEY COCHRANE'S MITT. Cochrane caught in over 1,400 games and five World Series and had four seasons in which he was the leading fielder among American League catchers.

Wide-grain, tight-grain, slim-handled or thick. Big-barreled, small-barreled, small-knobbed, end-cupped or non-cupped. Solid, two-toned, black, yellow or banded like a bee. The weapon of choice comes in infinite varieties, and even in the early days was customized whenever possible (and legal) to suit a certain player's swinging style. Early bats were considerably more substantial than today's equipment.

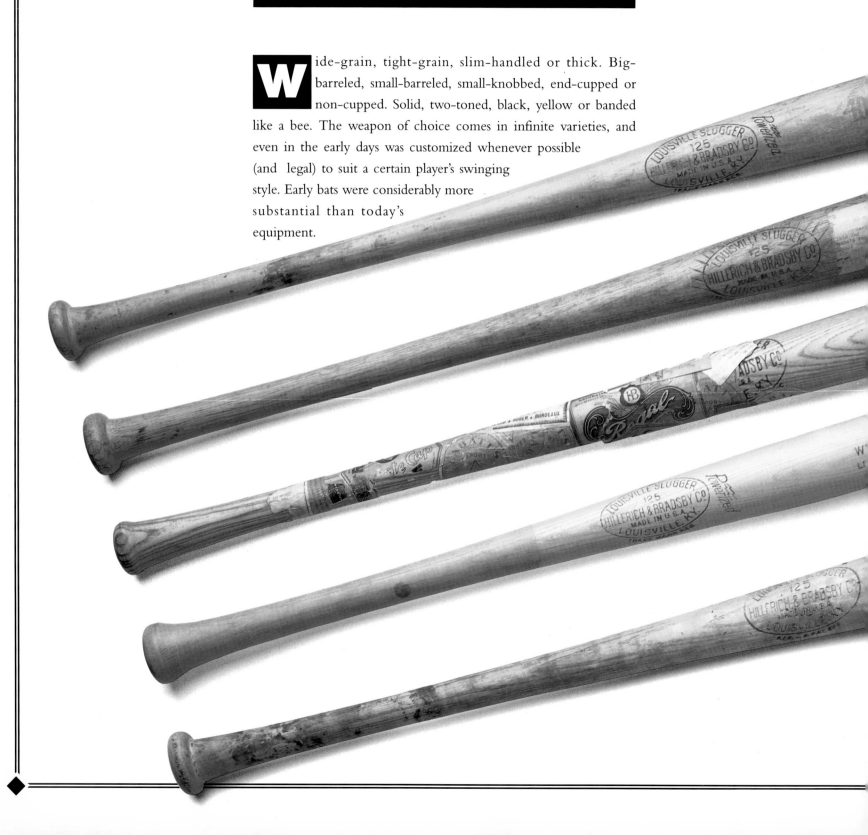

Averaging 36–43 ounces (versus the modern 32–33 ounces), these were big-nosed, fat-handled clubs suited to a generation of overgrown farm boys and field hands, bludgeons for big men who stepped up to the plate and walloped with solid intent. Many were made of hickory for durability, rather than the springier, modern choice of white ash, because bats back then were meant to take quite a bit more punishment. Today's habit of breaking two or three bats per game would have been considered bad business by early players – especially since the breaking of a bat in those days was thought to cause bad luck.

FROM LEFT TO RIGHT:

PETE BROWNING'S original Louisville Slugger.

HANK AARON'S bat.

DEL UNSER'S bat.

TONY GWYNN'S bat.

LEFT, TOP TO BOTTOM:

JOE DiMAGGIO'S bat.

BABE RUTH'S bat.

TRIS SPEAKER'S bat.

WEE WILLIE KEELER'S toothpick.

TED WILLIAMS' splinter.

LEFT: THE ONE AND ONLY. A 1915 Red Sox scorecard illustrates Babe's early pitching prowess.

BELOW: Bag and ball from Ruth's other power sport: bowling.

RIGHT: One of the few balls that didn't escape over the fence, signed with a flourish for a loyal Yankee fan.

LEFT: A box of winning underwear endorsed by Mr. Champion Nine.

BELOW: **"ONE SILVER DOLLAR,"** autographed.

BOTTOM: **THE MIGHTY GAUNTLET** of baseball's own "White Knight."

61

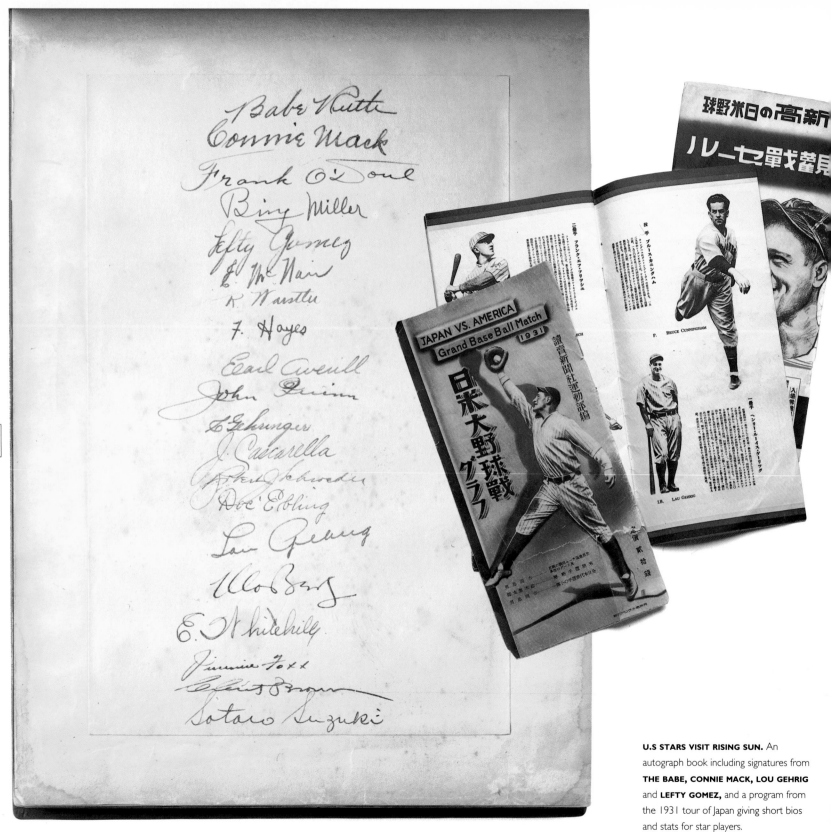

Babe Ruth
Connie Mack
Frank O'Doul
Bing Miller
Lefty Gomez
E. McNair
R. Warstler
F. Hayes
Earl Averill
John Quinn
C Gehringer
J. Cascarella
Robert Schroeder
Doc Ebling
Lou Gehrig
Moe Berg
E. Whitehill
Jimmie Foxx
Clint Brown
Sotaro Suzuki

U.S STARS VISIT RISING SUN. An autograph book including signatures from **THE BABE, CONNIE MACK, LOU GEHRIG** and **LEFTY GOMEZ,** and a program from the 1931 tour of Japan giving short bios and stats for star players.

TOOLS OF THE TRADE: MICKEY COCHRANE'S catcher's gear from his days with the **PHILADELPHIA ATHLETICS,** 1925–33. Out of his padding and up at bat, Mickey was struck in the head by a pitch on May 25, 1937, ending his career with a fractured skull – and a .320 average.

CLOCKWISE FROM LEFT: The working hands of **LUKE APPLING, WHITE SOX** shortstop; **HACK WILSON,** the **BROOKLYN DODGERS** bulldog, with size 18 collar and a size 6 shoe; and **HENRY "HEINIE" MANUSH** from **THE SENATORS,** a .330 hitter and the first player ever ejected from a Series game for snapping an umpire's bow tie.

ON THE **AIR**

The first nationally broadcast baseball game in America was the 1923 World Series between the Yankees and the Giants. The all–New York series (for the third time) was a rivalry guaranteed to pique the interest of fans far and near. Sure enough, thousands waited by the radio (which, in small towns, often belonged to the local barber) to "see" these historic games courtesy of the vivid verbalizations of Graham MacNamee. MacNamee, who abandoned a professional singing career earlier that year to pursue a job in the fledgling broadcast industry, became almost overnight "The Voice of Baseball." His riveting play-by-play descriptions (usually aided by a team of baseball writers who provided the groundwork on which his flowery prose could grow) would become a standard for over a decade of World Series. The enormous popularity of broadcast games was the very reason the leagues mostly discouraged radio, even going so far as to ban all broadcasts except the Series. The leagues feared that regular broadcasts would seriously reduce game attendance, a prophecy that television would, to a certain extent, fulfill some 20 years later.

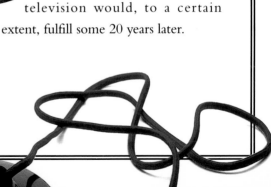

WAR SHIRTS.

LEFT: Jersey from 1927, belonging to notoriously tough **JOHN McGRAW,** who was honored that year with John McGraw Day at the Polo Grounds, commemorating his 25 years as the **GIANTS** manager.

BELOW: **DIZZY DEAN** of the **ST. LOUIS CARDINALS** wore this jersey in 1934, the year he won 30 games and led the NL in wins, strikeouts and shutouts.

WAR BONNET. FRANK SNYDER, a big Texan catcher who helped the **GIANTS** grab four straight pennants in 1921–24, wore this hat.

TOP: **"THE PRIDE AND JOY OF EVERY AMERICAN BOY."** A mail-away club package from the **KNOTHOLE LEAGUE,** a fan club sponsored by Goudey Gum Co.

CENTER: A **TICKET** from the **LOU GEHRIG** memorial game July 4, 1939 – possibly the most famous ceremony in baseball history and certainly one of the saddest. On that day, Gehrig announced his retirement to the world. In spite of his disease, he asserted, "Today, I consider myself the happiest man on the face of the earth."

BOTTOM: **LOU GEHRIG TRADING CARD.**

THE WELL-WORN GLOVE of "The Iron Horse," America's foremost first baseman, used through Gehrig's amazing record of 2,130 consecutive games.

ODD MAN OUT

Casey Stengel called him "the strangest man in baseball." Small wonder. With degrees in law, mathematics and linguistics, White Sox catcher Moe Berg seemed astonishingly qualified for his chosen profession. Berg would accumulate huge piles of books and magazines while on tour, but forbid anyone to read them because the books would "die" if handled improperly. Teammates were mostly baffled about how Berg survived 16 years in the majors. The mystery was further enhanced by his resoundingly mediocre batting average. It was so low that one local wit was prompted to proclaim, "He can speak 12 languages but can't hit in any of them." The heart of the secret was that Berg was a spy, one of the most important, in fact, in America at that time. He went to Japan with an all-star traveling team in the '30s with Babe Ruth and Lou Gehrig, and came back with a bag full of espionage photos. Out of his team uniform during World War II, he was one of the most respected atomic "watchers" in the business and was awarded the Medal of Freedom (right) for his vital information on Germany's top scientists. Of course no one but the government knew any of this. The rest of the world just figured he was playing out in left field.

RIGHT: THE DUTCH MASTER RELIC. Ball from **CINCINNATI REDS** pitcher **JOHNNY VANDER MEER'S** second consecutive no-hitter game in 1938. He struck out Leo Durocher of the Dodgers to win this game on June 15, in what was also the first night game played at Ebbets Field. The first no-hitter was against the Boston Bees on June 11. Vander Meer's record string of 21 no-hit innings will probably never be broken.

BELOW: TICKET from same game.

1924 WASHINGTON SENATORS received this medal from a team owner in honor of their first World Series championship, played against the Giants.

EARLY WHEATIES CEREAL BOX.
Celebrating 100 years of baseball and the historical importance of a good breakfast.

PASS FOR THE NEW YORK GIANTS.
Although very official looking, the pass only granted you entrance to the park – but not always a seat.

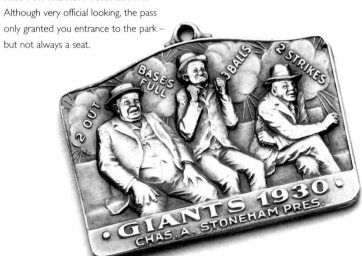

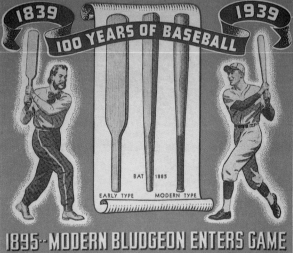

ABOVE LEFT: Sure-handed **WALLY PIPP** used this glove for 11 years with the **NY YANKEES,** until that fateful day in 1925 when Wally wasn't feeling well and took some time off. His substitute was a German-American rookie by the name of Lou Gehrig.

ABOVE RIGHT: Gorgeous George and his amazing glove. **GEORGE SISLER** of the **ST. LOUIS BROWNS** was undoubtedly one of the most elegant first basemen to ever dance the bag. His somewhat less-graceful looking glove is from 1920.

LEFT: Hardly used glove of **CHIEF MOSES J. YELLOWHORSE,** who joined the **PITTSBURGH PIRATES** in 1921 and parted company in 1922, or as they say, "he came up to the majors for a cup of coffee."

FALLEN FIELDS

The Polo Grounds, Ebbets Field, Forbes Field and a dozen other great parks are long since gone. These stadiums became the homes of legendary teams and the unique settings for landmark games. The Polo Grounds, residence to the Giants (1911–1956), the Yankees (1913–1922) and the Mets (1962–1963), is perhaps the Parthenon of all baseball stadiums. Famous for its odd horseshoe shape and virtually unreachable back wall, the Grounds was situated on Manhattan's East 159th Street, between the Harlem River and Coogan's Bluff. It held, at its peak, approximately 34,000 fans. It was demolished in 1964 after the completion of Shea Stadium, and a housing project and a playground stand in its place. Another New York late-great was Ebbets Field. Squashed into the Flatbush section of Brooklyn, this field had the distinction of being one of the rowdiest in either league. In the 1920s and 1930s a character named Hilda Chester brought her cowbell to each game and played enthusiastically while members of the Dodger Sym–phony (any fan with a free hand and some sort of musical instrument) woofed and tweeted the team to victory. In 1958 the Dodgers left for Los Angeles. Two years later, their famous park was razed for an apartment complex. Forbes Field was for 61 years the stronghold of the Pittsburgh Pirates. Forbes was also renowned as the scene of Babe Ruth's final career home run, on May 25, 1935, hit over the right field roof and off into history. Today a home plate memorial is all that remains on the site.

ABOVE: **NUMERAL** from **FORBES FIELD** scoreboard.

BELOW: **CERTIFICATE OF DEDICATION** for **EBBETS FIELD,** July 15, 1913.

The **STADIUM SEAT** used by **MRS. JOHN McGRAW,** wife of the dictatorial Giants manager, from the **NEW YORK POLO GROUNDS.**

The Officers and Directors of
The Brooklyn Ball Club
request the honor of your presence at the
Dedication of Ebbets Field
Bedford Avenue and Sullivan Street
Borough of Brooklyn, City of New York
Tuesday afternoon July the fifteenth
nineteen hundred and thirteen
at three o'clock
Brooklyn vs Chicago

TURN AND TURN AGAIN. The field is gone, but this **TURNSTILE** from the **NY POLO GROUNDS** survives, marking out the passage of 53 legendary years, one fan at a time.

1929 WORLD SERIES PROGRAM. The **CHICAGO CUBS** went up against the **PHILADELPHIA ATHLETICS** and lost. In the fifth game of the Series, with President and Mrs. Hoover looking on, the scoreless A's rallied at the bottom of the ninth and made three runs to take the game.

WAR AND THE REVOLUTION

Chapter

IV

WAR AND THE REVOLUTION

By 1934, time and too many sandwiches had caught up with the mighty Babe. After taking several salary cuts (by January 1934 he was down to a measly $35,000, less than half his peak rate), Babe was finally sold to Boston. This might have marked the end of an era, but New Yorkers being ever resourceful, Babe's space on the bench was hardly cold when a rookie by the name of Joe DiMaggio was signed on. DiMaggio in turn would pass the torch to Mickey Mantle in the '50s, keeping an unbroken line of legendary hitters in the dugout. Also ensuring the continued success of the Yankee dynasty was brilliant manager and language mangler Casey Stengel, who began his 12-year term with the not-so-brilliant announcement, "This is a big job, fellas, and I barely have had time to study it. In fact, I scarcely know where I am at." Stengel might have been careless with his verbs but he was meticulous about everything else. The scrapbook covering his entire 53 years with the game reads like the who's who and what's what of baseball.

From the mid-1930s to the late 1950s, baseball would undergo enormous growth and transformation, mirroring in many ways the economic, social and technical changes sweeping America. Baseball would make its own unique contributions to the war effort, and become an early crucible for social experiments involving women and blacks in the work force. While the Kenosha Comets program may not look like early feminism, and Jackie Robinson's 1947 integration of the Dodgers did not inspire immediate sweeping reforms, they were signs of a country in transition. America's post-Depression, East-to-West migration had gained considerable momentum by the 1950s, and is paralleled in the movement of teams such as the Dodgers and the Giants to California in 1959. And just as stunned New Yorkers could barely believe the home teams were leaving home, parents were watching the younger generation move out of old neighborhoods and away from families in America's new age of mobility. Radio broadcasts, initially banned by the leagues in the '30s, were attracting a wider, more diverse audience to the sport. But even the tremendously popular Harry Carey, with his vivid play-by-play announcements, couldn't rival the experience of a live game. Fans still flocked to the parks, still coveted souvenir pins and programs, still jumped for flies and fouls, and still lived for the chance to deliver in-person advice to the umpires.

Refinements in equipment continued, most noticeably in gloves, which became more complex throughout the '30s and '40s, resulting in the large, laced and webbed creations of the '50s. Uniforms were

also changing, with a movement towards lighter fabrics and more fitted shapes. Prime examples of this trend are found in the innovative silk jerseys of the 1948 Boston Braves and Stan Musial's streamlined #6. A new piece of defensive equipment, the batter's helmet, made its debut in the '40s. An early version, worn by Johnny Rucker of the New York Giants and designed to sidestep accusations of total sissiness, is cleverly disguised as a team cap with a concealed interior plastic shell. It saved pride but didn't do much for skulls, so more overt molded fiberglass designs were pursued. In spite of fierce resistance by players, batting helmets would become mandatory in the late '50s. With power pitchers like the Phillies' Robin Roberts hurling 95 mph balls on a regular basis, it was none too soon.

But in the season of 1941, most of this was still in the faraway future. It was the summer of DiMaggio's 56 consecutive-hit streak. Ted Williams raised his batting average to over .400 for the first time in a season. Stan Musial made his major league debut. And Brooklyn finally got it together and brought home the pennant, after two decades of blank behavior on the field. Then suddenly, war. The world's attention turned to other, more serious pursuits. In spite of President Roosevelt's historic "green light letter" of January 15, 1942, urging the leagues to keep playing, there really wasn't anyone left in the clubhouse. All the best young men were signed or signing up for the military. And so began the patchwork chronicles of baseball's war years, certainly some of the oddest teams and players ever to line up across a ballfield: a 15-

year-old pitcher, a one-armed outfielder, an all-St. Louis 1944 World Series and ladies in the dugout. Truly a time of weirdness for the sport. But baseball limped along, patching together clubs from whoever was available (and un-enlisted). By 1945 the war was over, but another battle had just begun. Cyclone Joe Williams, Cannonball Dick Redding, Cool Papa Bell, Martin Dihigo, Satchel Paige — brilliant

players of unquestioned ability – couldn't get anywhere near the leagues. You just didn't get asked if you happened to be black. Eighty-five years after the Emancipation Proclamation the only people free to play major league baseball were whites, the result of an unspoken agreement between owners. Even John McGraw, who was absolutely color-blind when it came to talent, couldn't get blacks on the Giants roster, in spite of several attempts to "pass" colored players as Indian or Cuban. This prohibition was ended by the determined and singularly brave Branch Rickey. In the face of fierce resistance, Rickey signed Jackie Robinson with the Dodgers in 1945. Rickey was met with everything from threats of player resignations to a rumored strike by the Cardinals in 1947, when they supposedly planned to quit the field rather than share it with a black player. Rickey and Robinson met every indignity with grace and with silence. There would be no fighting back, no incidents. Finally Ford Frick, the president of the National League, issued a statement early in 1947 that laid down the law in no uncertain terms:

"This is the United States of America and one citizen has as much right to play as another."

The struggle for integration could no longer be diverted or ignored. Two years later, in 1949, Jack Roosevelt Robinson was voted the National League's Most Valuable Player.

CHAPTER OPENER: YOGI BERRA, WHITEY FORD and **ERNIE BANKS** captured in 1950s plastic.

PAGE 74: BALL from 1940 All-Star game.

PAGE 75: JACKIE ROBINSON'S CAP from the 1955 **WORLD SERIES.**

ABOVE: HISTORIC PITCHING RUBBER from **YANKEE ALLIE REYNOLDS'** second no-hitter in the 1951 season. Both New York and Boston teams autographed the 24-inch-long, 45-pound block from Yankee Stadium for the winning pitcher.

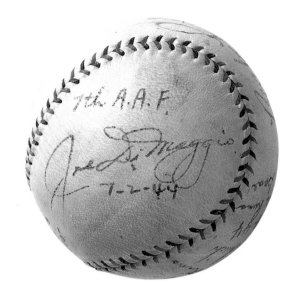

THE WHITE HOUSE
WASHINGTON

January 15, 1942.

My dear Judge:-

Thank you for yours of January fourteenth. As you will, of course, realize the final decision about the baseball season must rest with you and the Baseball Club owners -- so what I am going to say is solely a personal and not an official point of view.

I honestly feel that it would be best for the country to keep baseball going. There will be fewer people unemployed and everybody will work longer hours and harder than ever before.

And that means that they ought to have a chance for recreation and for taking their minds off their work even more than before.

Baseball provides a recreation which does not last over two hours or two hours and a half, and which can be got for very little cost. And, incidentally, I hope that night games can be extended because it gives an opportunity to the day shift to see a game occasionally.

As to the players themselves, I know you agree with me that individual players who are of active military or naval age should go, without question, into the services. Even if the actual quality of the teams is lowered by the greater use of older players, this will not dampen the popularity of the sport. Of course, if any individual has some particular aptitude in a trade or profession, he ought to serve the Government. That, however, is a matter which I know you can handle with complete justice.

Here is another way of looking at it -- if 300 teams use 5,000 or 6,000 players, these players are a definite recreational asset to at least 20,000,000 of their fellow citizens -- and that in my judgment is thoroughly worthwhile.

With every best wish,

Very sincerely yours,

Hon. Kenesaw M. Landis,
333 North Michigan Avenue,   Franklin D Roosevelt
Chicago,
Illinois.

PRESIDENT ROOSEVELT'S LETTER to the leagues, urging that baseball continue in spite of the war, for the morale of the country.

ST. LOUIS BROWNS HAT from the unlikeliest participants in the 1944 World Series which they lost to the St. Louis Cardinals four games to two.

ALL-STAR SOUVENIR PINS.

WHEN WOMEN WENT TO BAT

O f all the odd arrangements made to keep the game going during the war years, none was as revolutionary as the idea of a women's baseball league. Faced with the likely cancellation of major league baseball in the fall of 1942 due to a manpower shortage, Chicago Cubs owner Philip K. Wrigley had the idea to organize and promote women in the sport. After a brief spring training at Wrigley Field, the All-American Girls Softball League (as it was first called) went public with four teams: the Rockford Peaches, South Bend Blue Sox, Kenosha Comets and Racine Belles. By 1945, play was evolving to

more closely resemble baseball and the teams had renamed themselves the All-American Girls Professional Baseball League. Players were expected to embody the "highest ideals of womanhood," which included wearing short, flared dresses with satin boxer shorts underneath, and lipstick whenever a player went up to bat. Lessons in grooming and deportment were as much a part of the program as batting practice and base slides. In spite of all the emphasis on femininity in the field, by 1954, the league's last year, the ladies were playing near-regulation hardball, with full overhand pitching from a 60-foot distance.

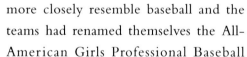

KENOSHA COMETS HAT and **YEARBOOK.**

MICKEY MANTLE'S immortal #7, pictured here on his "home" jersey. The YANKEES would retire the number in 1969 after 17 years of meritorious service.

HIDDEN PROTECTION in this 1941 **GIANTS CAP** belonging to **JOHNNY RUCKER,** the "Crabapple Comet," nephew of Nap. Plastic pads inserted inside a regular hat offered some safeguard to both skull and pride. This hat came in handy while Rucker led the NL in at-bats that year.

PROTOTYPE for the modern molded baseball helmet. This design, from the 1955 **PITTSBURGH PIRATES,** was fiberglass. It became obsolete upon the introduction of a stronger shell plastic known as **CYCOLAC** and the addition of ear flaps.

OUTLINE of **ROBIN ROBERTS'** big toe shows clearly through the reinforced end of his pitching shoes. He exerted considerable force on them while becoming the foremost pitcher in **PHILLIES** history, winning 20 games a season for six years in a row, 1950–55.

A **SEPARATE** LEAGUE

Negro leagues existed in America until 1960. For 40 years, they had a rich playing history, their own World Series and more than a few heroes. In spite of poor pay, impossible travel conditions and an almost complete lack of official recognition by the all-white (and restricted) major leagues, black players such as Cyclone Joe Williams, Cool Papa Bell, Cannonball Dick Redding, John Henry Lloyd and the great Satchel Paige performed with a brilliance that is still remembered. Recently, there has been a movement to include more of the Negro League players in the Baseball Hall of Fame; at present, seven have been inducted. The first organized major Negro baseball league was the Negro National League, formed in 1920. Other leagues such as the Negro Southern League, American Negro League and Eastern Colored League were formed and then repeatedly folded, some after only a few years. While there seemed to be enough players and a solid fan base, there was never enough money to support the various franchises. Cities who fielded teams were Baltimore, Chicago, Kansas City, New York and Philadelphia. Less regularly but also on the roster were Atlantic City, Birmingham, Cleveland, Detroit, Indianapolis, Memphis, Newark, Pittsburgh, St. Louis and Washington. The teams normally played between 50 and 80 games a season and their schedules were often arranged to allow member teams to play opposite white semi-pro teams, whom they usually defeated. Only 11 Black World Series were ever played, however, due to the constant dissolution of various leagues and franchises.

NEGRO LEAGUE TICKET.

COMISKEY PARK 35th St. and Shields Ave.
16th ANNUAL
**NATIONAL COLORED
ALL STAR
BASEBALL CLASSIC**
22
LOWER DECK BOX $3.00
Est. Price $2.50 Fed. Tax 50¢
43
3
7

SUNGLASSES from the very **'COOL' PAPA BELL.**

SATCHEL PAIGE'S SHOES, with reinforced pitching toe.

ROBERT "ROOSTER" SMITH'S SHOES.

LYMAN BOSTOCK SR.'S JACKET.

NEW YORK CUBAN STARS

NEWARK Eagles

PHILADELPHIA STARS

HOMESTEAD GRAYS

N.Y. BLACK YANKEES

NEGRO LEAGUE PENNANTS.

**STAN "THE MAN" MUSIAL'S ST. LOUIS
CARDINALS** jersey was as crisp and clean
as the man who wore it through a record
22 seasons.

ABOVE: The **BOSTON BRAVES** sported these silk jerseys for a short time in 1948 with the hopes that they would play cooler, but they never won player – or fan – approval.

LEFT: BOSTON RED SOX uniform that **TED WILLIAMS** wore during his last season of major league play, in which he batted .316. "The Splendid Splinter" hit one out of Fenway Park in his last at-bat in 1960.

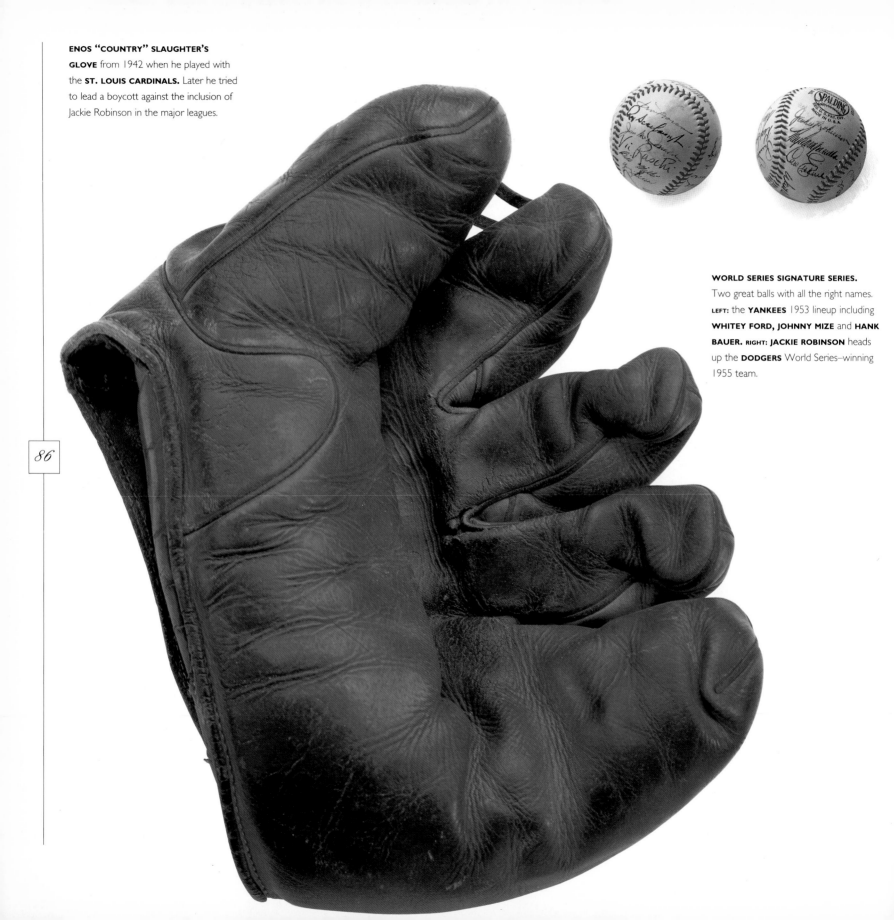

ENOS "COUNTRY" SLAUGHTER'S GLOVE from 1942 when he played with the **ST. LOUIS CARDINALS.** Later he tried to lead a boycott against the inclusion of Jackie Robinson in the major leagues.

WORLD SERIES SIGNATURE SERIES. Two great balls with all the right names. LEFT: the **YANKEES** 1953 lineup including **WHITEY FORD, JOHNNY MIZE** and **HANK BAUER.** RIGHT: **JACKIE ROBINSON** heads up the **DODGERS** World Series–winning 1955 team.

THE **LONELIEST JOB**

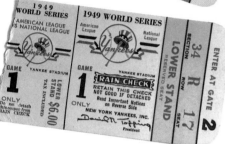

WORLD SERIES RING from 1955, the only year the **DODGERS** won the Series as a New York team.

As a major league manager once said about umpires, "Even when they're right, they're wrong." Considering the job entails an endless series of unpopular decisions, it's no wonder umpires often look so grim – it isn't easy being the only guy on the field that nobody's rooting for. Only recently have umpires banded together. The Major League Umpires Association, formed in 1968, went into action almost immediately to upgrade both salaries and stature, to implement certain practical changes (such as the sale of ballpark drinks in cups, eliminating the need for officials to duck dangerous bottles), and to strengthen the respect accorded to the profession by the leagues. The "umpire's umpire" was Bill Klem, who stood in the National League from 1905 to 1940 as "the Old Arbitrator." Most of the arm signals used today were invented by Klem, who oversaw home plate for 18 World Series. Also notable among the early umps were Jocko Conlan, who started as a mediocre player with the White Sox and became an umpire unexpectedly when one of

the working officials passed out from heatstroke and Jocko was asked to step in and finish the game, and Russell "Lena" Blackburne, who in 1938 discovered a secret source of extraordinarily fine mud that is still used today as the official goo for taking the slick off factory-new baseballs. In addition to overseeing the condition of the balls and the field, calling pitches and plays, and enforcing rules, an umpire's duties also include the periodic dusting off of bases. There is an unwritten law that when an umpire cleans home plate, he never does so with his fanny to the crowd. This bit of gentlemanly tradition is characteristic of the "umpire code."

JOCKO CONLAN'S WHISKBROOM.

BILL KLEM'S INDICATOR.

HOLY COW! AWARD presented to Chicago announcer **HARRY CARAY** in honor of outstanding sportscasting and frequent bovine references.

Fans' admiration shows for **DUKE SNIDER** of the **DODGERS** and for **PARKWAY FIELD.**

SILVER TROPHY BAT presented to **GEORGE KELL** of the **DETROIT TIGERS** in 1949, for winning the American League batting championship. Kell's batting average was just .0002 above Ted Williams', who had led until the last week of the season.

"OLE CASE"

OAKLAND ACORNS
Pacific Coast Champions
1948

Fan buttons celebrating **PEE WEE REESE**, nicknamed after a marble, and for keeping the home team home.

STENGEL'S MEMORIES in an embossed leather scrapbook. Bulging with newspaper clippings and photographs, it spans an amazing 53-year career as player and manager with the **DODGERS, BRAVES, YANKEES, PHILLIES, GIANTS, PIRATES** and **METS.** The year he began his collection – 1948 – he led the **OAKLAND OAKS** to a first-place position in the Pacific Coast League.

BROOKLYN DODGERS

BANNER from the 1958 **BROOKLYN DODGERS** featuring their longtime mascot, **EMMETT KELLY.**

Modern Times

Chapter

V

MODERN TIMES

One sunny afternoon in a baseball legend, Ernie Banks said "Let's play two!" and everyone understood exactly. Because the weather was beautiful. Because scooping up those ground balls made players feel as graceful as Fred Astaire. Because, like us, Banks was so in love with the game he couldn't wait to play again. This spontaneous enthusiasm is the demarcation between the early ages and the modern era. Money had absolutely nothing to do with "Let's play two!" Lawyers did not negotiate, nor did accountants advise. No contract issues were discussed. It was simply a glorious day and a lot of fun and Ernie didn't think once about the commercial possibilities of another nine innings. This was a moment of pure baseball at a time before money and business interests and lawsuits made it less of a "game."

To many, the '50s and '60s really belong to two names, Mr. Mays and Mr. Mantle. Willie Howard Mays came up to the Giants by way of their Minnesota farm team with an already notable .477 average. It was in the field, though, that his real genius would be realized. Mays operated on a fairly simple, ultimately unbeatable principle: always get the ball. Whether it took a leap, a slide, a full, dirt belly flop – whatever. On one occasion, he even took a line drive in deep center with his bare hand. Returning to the dugout, Mays expected some congratulations from the team for his unheard-of play. Instead, he got the silent treatment. Unable to accept that the whole club wasn't properly amazed, Mays couldn't resist confronting his manager: "Leo, didn't you see what I did out there?" To which Leo Durocher replied, "No. So you'll just have to go out there and do it again before I'll believe it." Mays was truly a Renaissance man of baseball. He ran bases with both speed and smarts. He played center-field brilliantly and consistently. His enthusiasm for the game, and life in general, endeared him to players and fans. Mays' ability to pull off seemingly impossible center-field plays would continue through the '50s on into the '60s. In 1965 he would join Ruth, Foxx, Kiner and Mantle as the only players with more than one 50-home-run season. And in 1971, when Mays put his foot down on the scarred home plate (pictured on page 94) and scored his 1,950th run, he set a new National League record.

Like Mays, Mickey Mantle came up in 1951. A switch-

CHAPTER OPENER: **HENRY AARON'S #44 ATLANTA BRAVES UNIFORM.**

PAGE 92: **61 in '61.** The famed 61st home run ball hit by **ROGER MARIS** of the **NEW YORK YANKEES.** In one swat, this ball shattered Babe Ruth's legendary "60 in a season" and set a new major league record.

PAGE 93: **FLEETING FASHION.** Assorted jerseys in eye-popping polyester. Fan reaction was overwhelmingly negative. In fact, the **PHILLIES'** cranberry concoction was retired after only one game.

HISTORIC HOME. On May 30, 1971 **WILLIE MAYS,** playing for the **SAN FRANCISCO GIANTS,** stepped on this plate from Candlestick Park and scored his 1,950th run. It was the new National League record.

hitter of awesome profile, Mantle was a multi-talented offensive threat. Nicknamed the "Commerce Comet" (for his hometown of Commerce, Oklahoma), Mantle blazed his way out of the minors and onto the Yankee roster with the kind of fanfare that tends to thoroughly irritate the press. Perceived as arrogant, with more bluster than talent, he was not fully appreciated in the early years. But in 1960, the press coverage changed and people recognized that Mantle played in almost constant pain; his knees were bad and getting worse. In spite of this he would play until 1968 and achieve 536 career home runs, establishing World Series records for home runs (18), RBIs (40) and runs (42).

The '60s were a time of change and turmoil for the world at large and America in particular, and the '70s were even more volatile. Although baseball remained a game proud to have resisted change since the turn of the century, and its rules and regulations were relatively intact, records were falling. The first and possibly most sacred statistic to bite the dust was the Babe's record of 60 home runs in a season (1927). One of those highly cherished and seemingly immortal achievements, the Babe's big one was broken in 1961 when Roger Maris blew everything apart with 61 homers. Old-timers everywhere said it felt like the sky had fallen. Next came the Babe's seemingly untouchable 714 lifetime homers; on April 8, 1974, Henry Aaron hit his 715th, backing Babe a little farther off the plate. Then there was the daunting Ty Cobb's 96 stolen bases in a single season. It held until Maury Wills thieved his way to 104 in 1962, only to be out-stolen by Lou Brock with 118 in 1974, who in turn was passed by Rickey Henderson with an incredible 130 bases in 1982. And finally, the long-standing record of Bob Feller's 348 strikeouts in a season (1946) was blown away in 1965 by Sandy Koufax (382) and again, in 1973, when Nolan Ryan sent 383 out from the mound. Nothing was sacred anymore.

The traditional look of the game was undergoing radical changes as well. Polyester suits in body-hugging designs and shrieking color schemes were finding their way onto the field, and tank top ensembles put a severe, if temporary, dent in the style of the sport. While drooping mustaches had been popular in baseball from the very first days, long hair was a new twist. The mid and late '60s were also a time of great expansion, with new teams like the San Diego Padres, Houston Astros and Montreal Expos appearing – and in some cases, like the Seattle Pilots, disappearing – seemingly overnight. This was also a time of intense media inspection and dissection of players and the game. Negative news involving players and their fast-lane lifestyles became more prevalent as reporters became generally less respectful of the heroes. Then, as if to further emphasize the new forces emerging in baseball, 1972 brought an unprecedented and certainly unexpected event: the first general players strike. Because the subject up for discussion concerned the amount of money club owners should contribute to the players' pension fund, the strike redirected the public's attention away from who the opening day pitchers would be toward questions like how much do owners offer and how much do players earn. What was a game, a simple game, had suddenly become big business. In 1977, when the news that Reggie Jackson, Mike Schmidt and Joe Rudi were making over half a million dollars got more press than their batting averages, the old feelings about the game just seemed to have slipped a little. But in spite of the commercial changes, the greatest reward of baseball comes simply when the game is played well and loved fiercely. This is what keeps pulling us back to the park, this and our belief that legends can still happen right there on the diamond; men can be heroes, at least for a play, and somewhere out there an endless and wonderful summer is waiting for us all.

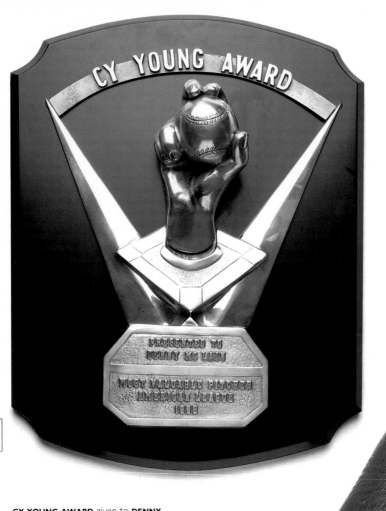

CY YOUNG AWARD given to **DENNY McLAIN** in 1968. Brash, flamboyant, then arrested, McLain went from leading the American League in pitching and two Cy Young Award honors to bankruptcy and conviction on drug and racketeering charges. The award was sold to a collector when McLain fell on hard times.

SANDY'S SPECIAL. The 1962 no-hitter ball that sent the Mets home moping. **KOUFAX** pitched one no-hitter game each season from 1962 to 1965, ending in a 1-0 perfect game against the Cubs on September 9, 1965.

FIRST GLOVE. Early '50s high school glove belonging to **SANDY KOUFAX,** brilliant pitcher for 12 seasons with the **DODGERS.** In his early years in the majors, Koufax was a power thrower with control problems, but he would polish his pitch to Hall of Fame status in the last 5 years of his 10-year career. An ailing arm forced his retirement after the 1966 season.

LEFT: 104TH STOLEN. In 1962 **MAURY WILLS** slid feet first into this base and a new league record. He was the first person to steal over 100 bases in a single season.

BELOW: SOUVENIR PINS.

LEFT TO RIGHT: **MANIFEST DESTINY.**
CONNIE MACK'S original **ATHLETICS OF**
PHILADELPHIA (1901–54) moved briefly
to **KANSAS CITY** (1955–67) before
becoming a West Coast franchise in
1968, the **OAKLAND A'S.**

WORLD SERIES TICKETS.

HOT SUMMER NIGHTS gave rise to the tank-top look in the 1970s. **REGGIE JACKSON** wore his **#9 A'S** jersey with a T-shirt underneath, as did most other players.

JERRY KOOSMAN wore this shirt while helping the 1969 **METS** achieve miracle status in the World Series. After seven years of losing — the Mets had never finished higher than ninth place — they finally became champions by beating the highly favored Baltimore Orioles, four games to one. Koosman had a record of 17–9 and, along with Tom Seaver, was among the Mets' top pitchers.

WOULD-BE WINNERS. Any team with a shot at the **WORLD SERIES** must print their tickets well in advance. Sure to go all the way in '64, the **PHILLIES** went out the window instead, experiencing the greatest collapse in baseball history by losing 10 games in a row at the season's end.

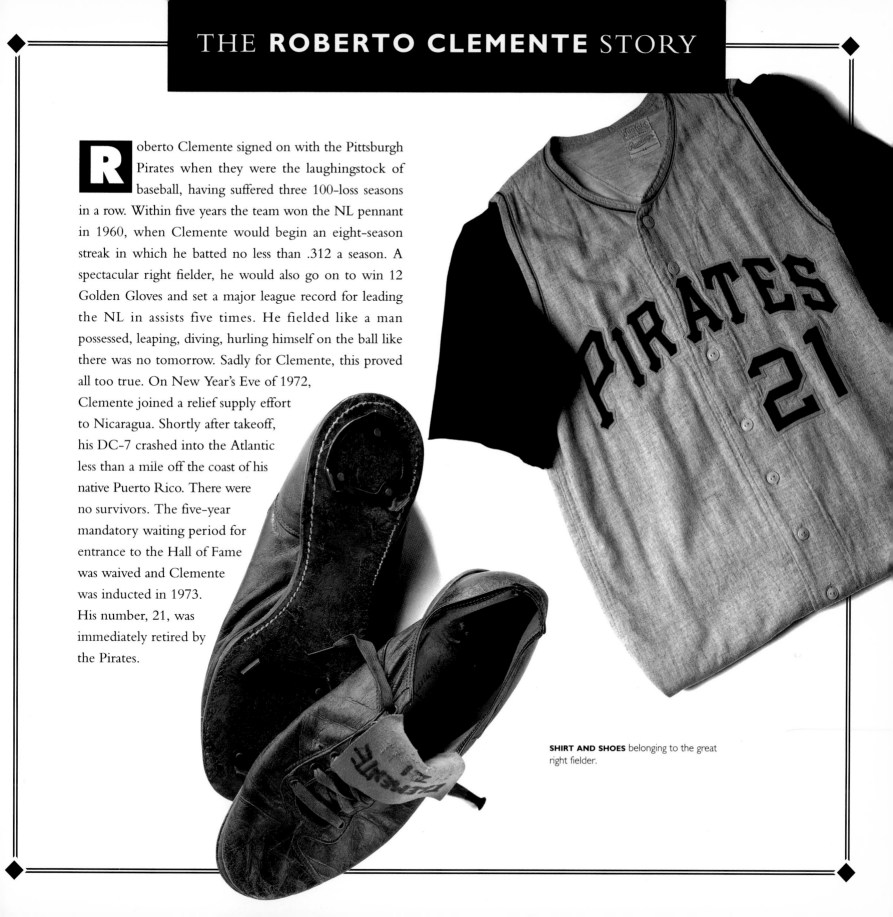

Roberto Clemente signed on with the Pittsburgh Pirates when they were the laughingstock of baseball, having suffered three 100-loss seasons in a row. Within five years the team won the NL pennant in 1960, when Clemente would begin an eight-season streak in which he batted no less than .312 a season. A spectacular right fielder, he would also go on to win 12 Golden Gloves and set a major league record for leading the NL in assists five times. He fielded like a man possessed, leaping, diving, hurling himself on the ball like there was no tomorrow. Sadly for Clemente, this proved all too true. On New Year's Eve of 1972, Clemente joined a relief supply effort to Nicaragua. Shortly after takeoff, his DC-7 crashed into the Atlantic less than a mile off the coast of his native Puerto Rico. There were no survivors. The five-year mandatory waiting period for entrance to the Hall of Fame was waived and Clemente was inducted in 1973. His number, 21, was immediately retired by the Pirates.

SHIRT AND SHOES belonging to the great right fielder.

LEFT: **WILLIE MAYS UNIFORM** and **BAT** from the late '60s.

BELOW: **THE GIFTED HAND OF WILLIE MAYS.** Mays' preeminence as a center fielder was supported by stats (career total, 7,095 putouts) and the routine performance of seemingly impossible plays. Mays was famous for pulling in unreachable flies and for nailing long throws to the plate, once from an amazing 430 feet, with consistent accuracy.

BOTTOM: **BATTING HELMET** from 1967–68, also belonging to Mays. Note the large crack at ear level.

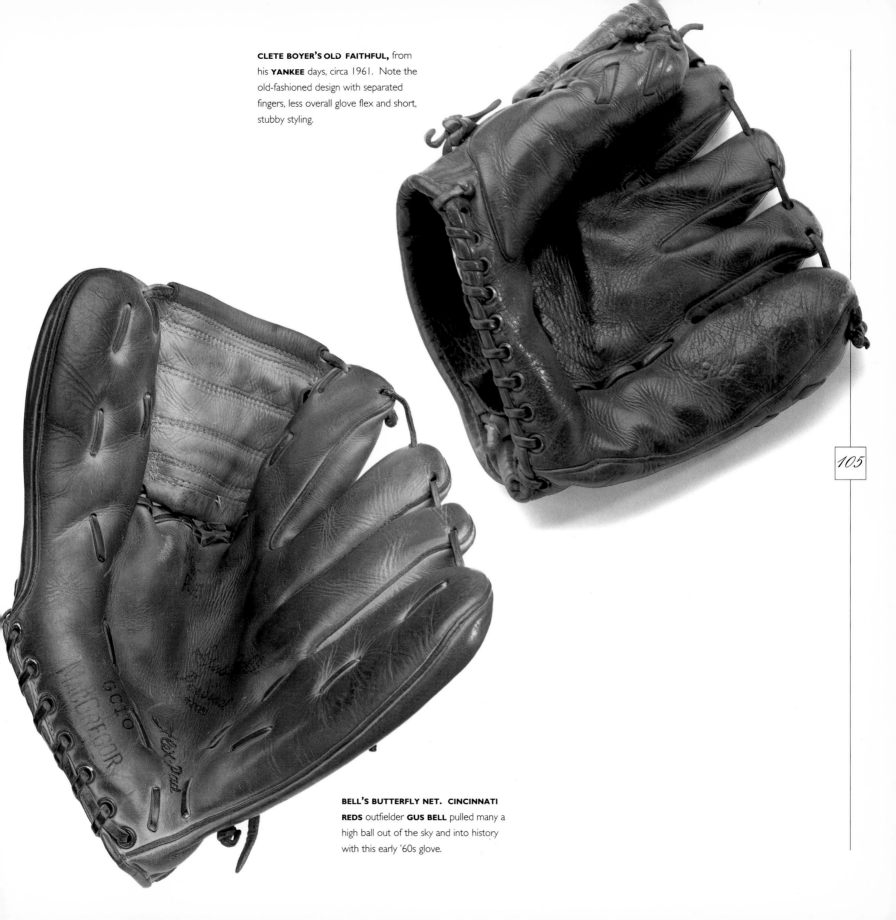

CLETE BOYER'S OLD FAITHFUL, from his **YANKEE** days, circa 1961. Note the old-fashioned design with separated fingers, less overall glove flex and short, stubby styling.

BELL'S BUTTERFLY NET. CINCINNATI REDS outfielder **GUS BELL** pulled many a high ball out of the sky and into history with this early '60s glove.

WELL-HEELED NOLAN RYAN became baseball's first million-dollar-a-year player when he signed with the **HOUSTON ASTROS** in 1980. The shoes are from this period (1980–88), and are extraordinarily scuffed in the toe area from Nolan's drag-and-pivot pitcher's stance.

23 SKIDDOO. Shoes belonging to **RYNE SANDBERG,** of the famous rookie "blunder trade" that the Phillies are still regretting. Sandberg was packed off to the **CUBS** and a future filled with MVPs, Golden Gloves and All-Star Games.

THE COWBOY WITH RED SOX. Gun, holster and hat given to Boston shortstop **CARL YASTRZEMSKI** by singer/actor Gene Autry. The occasion was Yastrzemski's retirement from the majors in 1983 after 23 proud years, which included 3,419 hits and 452 homers.

THE **JAPANESE LEAGUE**

Baseball has been a favorite pastime in Japan almost as long as it has in America. The first teams were organized in 1869 when Catholic missionary Horace Wilson brought the game to the Far East. The extraordinary popularity of visiting American players such as Babe Ruth, Lou Gehrig and Joe DiMaggio led to the organization of a professional league in 1936. For all the similarities in official rules and regulations, Japanese baseball does have several rather distinct deviations. Players bow respectfully to the umpire. Upon striking out, the Japanese batter smiles politely and returns quietly to the bench. Foul balls that land in the stands are immediately returned to the umpires. No game may extend past 10 p.m. Teams are owned by major corporations and don't owe their allegiance to a city. Due to the strong sense of consensus and the community rather than the individual, Japanese players would consider it vulgar and selfish to engage in salary disputes. In spite of the strong team identity, top players are treated with a reverence that even American superstars don't command. Home run champion Sadaharu Oh needed bodyguards to protect him from fervent fans and was paid a quarter of a million dollars in the mid-1970s. In spite of the lure of lucrative U.S. contracts, only one Japanese player has ever gone to the American majors. Masanori Murakami, a left-handed pitcher went to the San Francisco Giants in the '60s, but quickly returned home to Japan. After all, how could anyone seriously play ball in a country where they kick dirt at the umpire and spit all sorts of strange things onto the base paths?

LEFT: YUTAKA FUKUMOTO'S GOLDEN SLIPPERS awarded for 1,000 successful stolen bases.

ABOVE: TIDDLY-WINKS featuring Japanese baseball stars. **RIGHT: "HOT AND DISTANCE,"** jersey and bat belonging to **SADAHARU OH.**

TWENTY YEARS OF THE BEST. BROOKS ROBINSON of the **BALTIMORE ORIOLES,** unquestionably one the greatest defensive third basemen ever, used this glove in over 2,500 games during the '60s and '70s. Nicknamed "Hoover" for his talent at vacuuming up balls, Robinson specialized in dazzling defensive plays.

UNUSUAL HEADGEAR because Robinson was famous for wearing a trademarked short-billed **BATTING HELMET.** This longer variety was used in spring training and shows evidence of an exceedingly rough pre-season.

FAR RIGHT: THE ONE THAT BROKE THE BABE. Batting order for that momentous day of April 8, 1974, when **HANK AARON,** batting fourth, hit his 715th homer, which knocked Babe Ruth out of first place in the record books.

BOTTOM RIGHT: GEORGIA'S FINEST. Driver's license belonging to one **HENRY LOUIS AARON,** professionally known as ''Hammerin' Hank.'' A fan at the DMV spotted this unlikely souvenir when it was turned in for renewal.

RIGHT: HANK AARON'S WORLD SERIES RING.

BELOW: HISTORIC HELMET, worn by **HANK AARON** during the 1966 season.

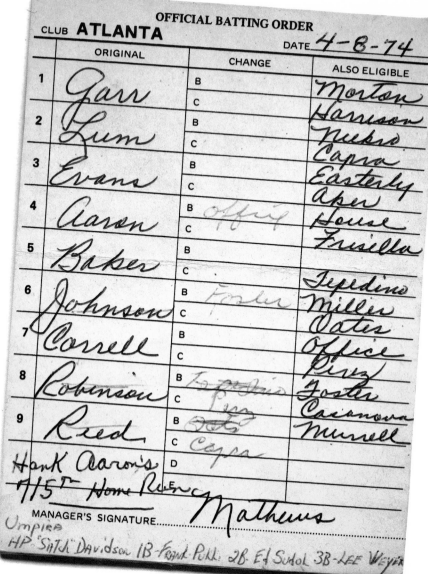